The Home Visitor's Manual

the home visitor's manual

Tools and Strategies for Effective Interactions with Family Child Care Providers

SHARON WOODWARD

DONNA C. HURLEY

Published by Redleaf Press
10 Yorkton Court
St. Paul, MN 55117
www.redleafpress.org

First edition 2010
Cover design by Jim Handrigan
Interior typeset in ITC Galliard and designed by Mayfly Design
Printed in the United States of America

17 16 15 14 13 12 11 10   1 2 3 4 5 6 7 8

Library of Congress Cataloging-in-Publication Data
Woodward, Sharon.
  The home visitor's manual : tools and strategies for effective interactions with family child care
providers / Sharon Woodward and Donna C. Hurley.—1st ed.
      p. cm.
  Includes bibliographical references.
  ISBN 978-1-60554-016-0 (alk. paper)
 1. Family day care—United States. 2. Early childhood education—United States. I. Hurley, Donna C.
II. Title.
  HQ778.63.W663 2011
  353.536—dc22
                              2009038101

FSC
Mixed Sources
Product group from well-managed
forests and other controlled sources
Cert no. SW-COC-002283
www.fsc.org
© 1996 Forest Stewardship Council

Printed on acid-free paper

*We dedicate this book to all the hardworking,
professional individuals who visit family child care homes
every day. We applaud your wonderful work.*

The Home Visitor's Manual

To our respective families, for their continued patience and support.

To all the people at Redleaf Press who have been so helpful and enthusiastic about this endeavor, with a special thank you to Deanne Kells, a wonderful editor.

To all the family child care providers who have graciously allowed us into their homes in order for us to develop our skills.

Introduction

As individuals who have collectively worked in the field of early childhood education for more than eighty years, we are pleased to welcome you to *The Home Visitor's Manual*.

Who This Manual Is For

In developing this book, we thought it important to identify all the groups of individuals who would find this manual a useful resource. What it eventually came down to was identifying all the people who visit homes where licensed child care takes place. As a result, we have chosen to use the term *home visitor* in a very literal way. The generic skills included in this book are designed to benefit anyone who visits a family child care home for the purposes of inspection, monitoring, evaluation, support, accountability, technical assistance, or investigation.

This book is for you if you visit family child programs in one of the following roles:

- Licenser
- Social worker
- Early intervention professional
- Food program monitor
- Family child care system representative
- Head Start personnel
- Child Development Associate (CDA) monitor
- Accreditation and environmental rating scale observer

In talking with providers throughout the United States, we quickly learned that a great number and variety of professionals visit family child care settings at one time or another. Identifying all the groups of professionals who visit family child care environments allowed us to create strategies that best serve all the professionals involved in this type of home visiting.

Why We Wrote This Manual

Home visitors face many challenges, dealing daily with a great variety of personalities, environments, and problems—each one as unique as the individual provider. This manual is written to equip home visitors with the skills and tools necessary to convey their messages in a manner that is acceptable and effective. Our hope is that this will result in home visits that are safe, positive, supportive, and motivationally interactive.

In conducting home visits for the purposes of social work, state licensing, monitoring, or investigating complaints, we have found there is no magic formula for successfully addressing individuals in their homes. We have conducted home visits in the inner-city, rural areas, suburbs, public housing, and affluent neighborhoods. In addition, we have provided child care orientations, assisted families with child care issues, and presented trainings at conferences, workshops, and in homes. Through the years, we have experienced many different and diverse situations and have dealt with an interesting variety of personalities. One thing we have learned is that when you are dealing with children and families, there is no end to the unique situations that can and do occur. This manual presents a variety of skills that will prepare the home visitor to meet these challenges successfully.

In preparation for the writing of this manual, we took an in-depth look at home visiting and identified areas in which we personally had experienced difficulty. In addition, we sent questionnaires to forty individuals who visit family child care homes to identify common situations and a wide variety of problems. From the responses to our questionnaire as well as our personal experience, we identified a series of relevant skills that we feel will benefit every home visitor. Those skills are what this manual is all about.

Importance of Home Visits
. . . .

We cannot emphasize enough how much the success of home visits can mean. Often home visits are required for providers to participate in state and federal programs. Home visitors who have the skills to connect with providers and bring them support and guidance help retain the participation of many qualified providers in these programs. The health and safety of young children as well as the quality of child care can be greatly influenced by an effective home visitor.

Most states have programs that reimburse family child care providers (and centers) for child care services given to parents who are income eligible or receive other types of assistance. These programs allow parents to go to school and/or work, giving them the opportunity to become self-sufficient. The child care reimbursement programs require an accounting of the services being reimbursed. Most programs require a home visitor to monitor the attendance and required services given to the child and family.

Yet in many of these programs, there has been a consistent reduction in enrollment. For example, participation in the Child and Adult Care Food Program (CACFP) nationwide has steadily declined. In 1996, 194,710 family child care homes participated; in 2007, 141,985—a drop of 52,725 homes, or 27.1 percent. The CACFP program is particularly important to feeding income-eligible children. Often these are the only nutritious meals many of these children receive. When providers were asked why they dropped out of these programs, the most prevalent answer was this: *Providers felt the home visits were invasive, and they did not like the way the home visitor enforced the regulations and requirements.* Clearly, the success of important programs like CACFP, for example, depends a great deal upon good working relationships between home visitors and providers.

Why Home Visitors Need Support
. . . .

Home visitors may find themselves in conflicting situations when parents and providers want to overlook some regulations. For example, your child care regulations may state that a baby must be on the same floor level as the provider at all times. A mother may want the provider to put her baby down to sleep in an upstairs bedroom because she feels the baby will sleep longer in a quiet room. Your job as a home visitor is to reinforce compliance with any applicable regulations. You represent your agency; you are also the person the providers and, on occasion, parents get to know, because you are in providers' homes on a regular basis. Whatever agency you work for, it usually has a mission statement that includes training, motivation, and support. If you are unaware of your organization's mission statement or your organization does not have one, you may want to address this with your supervisor. Administrators generally ask you to be respectful of the provider's home, to be encouraging and supportive when appropriate, and to foster a team spirit when working with the provider or parent. In reality, you are often asked to go into the provider's home in a regulatory capacity to investigate a problem or complaint or to implement a corrective action plan. It can be very uncomfortable to tell a provider that she needs to pay more attention to cleanliness, meal patterns, or unsafe conditions in the home. Even though you may be very knowledgeable about nutrition, child development, state regulations, and documentation requirements, you may experience difficulty in effectively getting tough messages across.

Administrators will find value in this manual by recognizing the important position home visitors hold in their organization. The home visitor represents the values and goals of your organization when interacting with providers and families. When home visitors have the skills to handle diverse situations, the results will become evident as you observe providers who are better trained, more satisfied, and receptive to furthering the goals of fostering quality care.

Often family child care providers appear more independent and knowledgeable than in the past. Providers today have access to many high-quality training sessions that were not available years ago. Today's trainings stress professionalism and assist providers in learning how to operate their own individual child care businesses. Operating a family child care business gives the provider freedom and independence. Even though state health and safety regulations exist, the provider is, for the most part, her own boss. Home visitors can play an important role in educating providers in the setup and operation of their family child care programs.

Most home visitors have the safety and well-being of children as their first priority. Yet it is sometimes difficult to balance the various regulatory and contractual requirements with the goal of supporting and encouraging a provider to maintain quality standards. Our goal is to assist you in the development of skills presented in this manual, which will lead you to interact with others in a productive and successful way so you can effectively educate, support, and model high-quality standards in child care.

Using This Manual

This manual is a reference guide. It is set up in modules. Each module discusses the skills you need to handle specific situations that may occur during your visits. Home visits are only one part of your job. This manual demonstrates how important preparation and follow-up are. In fact, they are often the keys to a successful visit.

All of the skills in this manual require *practice, practice, practice*. Keeping the manual handy and referring to it often will help you to master these skills. Use the manual as a reference for the following situations:

- Preparing to address a difficult situation
- Experiencing hostility in dealing with a provider
- Trying to motivate an unresponsive provider
- Fostering a team spirit between yourself and a provider
- Experiencing frustration because your message is not being heard
- Feeling unsafe in a particular environment
- Trying to solve a problem
- Delivering an unpleasant and difficult message

How the Manual Is Organized

Each module in this manual is designed to stand alone. This allows you to refer to a specific module that addresses a particular situation. Each module begins with an overview and learning objectives, followed by a case study demonstrating the skills used by home visitors on the job. Modules also include self-examination activities and useful checklists that help you prepare for and follow up on home visits. Real examples throughout each module help you put together ideas and identify ways to apply the skills discussed. Use these examples to relate to actual experiences in the field and to evaluate your performance in similar situations.

Module 1

Accept the Full Role of a Home Visitor

Module Description

Entering anyone's home for the purpose of determining accountability is a difficult task. When a monitor enters a provider's home and finds it necessary to give critical feedback, even the most professional home visitor, not to mention the family child care provider can become stressed. In this initial training module, we look at the many roles of a home visitor. After all, before attempting to develop skills that will assist you in doing your job, you must determine exactly what your job description includes.

Your employer has specific expectations about your job duties, and the clients you visit also have expectations about your responsibilities to them. This module identifies four roles that reflect the job duties of a large majority of individuals visiting family child care homes:

- Communicator
- Quality assurance inspector
- Public relations manager
- Role model

For the roles of communicator, quality assurance inspector, and a public relations manager, we identify strategies for effectively completing your home visit with an emphasis on client retention. Last, the responsibility of a role model is examined. This section identifies effective strategies for modeling relevant and professional behaviors.

Understanding your roles and the job expectations attached to those roles allows you to choose the appropriate skill training to enhance your professional development and do your job more effectively.

Learning Objectives

- Value the many roles you take on while performing your job duties as a home visitor.
- Be comfortable talking to clients and your supervisors.
- Understand the importance of objective evaluations of the home-based child care programs you visit.
- Effectively communicate your organization's mission statement.
- Retain clients.
- Have a positive effect on the clients you visit.

. . . .

Case Study

Home visitor Anna arrives at a provider's house for an unannounced visit. In many ways, Anna has been dreading coming to this home because she anticipates this visit will be difficult and time consuming.

When Anna enters the home, she is immediately greeted by the provider, who appears frazzled and more than a little frustrated. The provider is obviously upset about Anna's unexpected visit and exhibits defensive behavior. Her body language is tense and her tone of voice is strained. The provider's demeanor seems to be affecting the children as well, because they also appear uncomfortable.

Anna, because she has reviewed the file before making the visit, is aware that this client has expressed dissatisfaction in the past. The client's concerns have included what she considers to be mistrustful and accusatory policies by Anna's organization. Anna's unannounced visit seems to have confirmed the client's worst suspicions.

Anna understands it is to her advantage to keep this visit on track. She also realizes that this client needs and deserves an opportunity to communicate her concerns. In Anna's role as a *communicator,* she politely asks the client to explain her issues. In preparing for this visit, Anna has allowed for extra time, so she is comfortable giving the client the opportunity to talk. Anna listens attentively while using her communication skills to steer the conversation when it veers off course. At the conclusion of the client's comments, Anna assures her that she has been heard and that her concerns will be accurately communicated to Anna's supervisors.

As a *quality assurance inspector,* Anna performs her required assessment, using efficient and time-saving data collection tools. She does this while demonstrating that although the client may have concerns, Anna nonetheless has an obligation to perform her required assignments. She demonstrates by her speech and demeanor that her evaluation will be conducted fairly and consistently.

Anna performs as a *public relations manager* by offering helpful resource material specifically targeted to this client's needs. In doing so, Anna demonstrates that this visit is important and worth preparing for. While performing her assessment, Anna reinforces all the positive and appropriate things the provider is doing, along with areas in which targeted technical assistance may be helpful. Because of her advance preparations, Anna can answer the client's questions credibly and accurately. She also works at helping this provider understand the goal of quality child care shared by the provider and Anna's organization.

In fulfilling her responsibility as an appropriate *role model,* Anna maintains a calm demeanor even when the provider does not. Anna focuses appropriately on the purpose of the visit and demonstrates good organizational skills by coming prepared and ready to begin. She presents herself as a professional and conducts her visits professionally. This includes her appearance as well as her demonstrated respect for the client and the client's child care setting. Through modeling, Anna introduces behaviors that will help the client operate a successful business.

· · · · · · · · ·

Communicator

Regulatory and contractual information that providers need to operate their businesses effectively as well as legally very often comes straight from you. Unfortunately, the message you convey is not always the message a client wants to hear. As a result, your ability to communicate information, including unwelcome information, in a clear and understandable manner can greatly contribute to the success of the home-based businesses you visit. Whether they want to or not, providers must operate within the boundaries established by the authorities who oversee them. This makes your role as a communicator a very important one. You have an obligation to communicate information, and you have an implied obligation to make sure the client understands the information you have communicated. That kind of assurance only comes when you use effective communication strategies.

Presenting yourself as a proficient communicator is arguably one of the most important roles you will assume as a home visitor. In subsequent modules, strategies for successful communication will be discussed. These strategies have been developed specifically for individuals visiting caregivers in their homes. In this module, we present the basic requirements demanded in your role as a communicator.

Certainly one of your primary obligations when communicating information is to actually know what you're talking about. You are not only required to communicate information—you are required to communicate *accurate* information. You need to know and understand any regulations or contractual requirements related to your home visits. When a client asks a question that you are unable to answer with confidence, it's essential that you are able to obtain accurate information quickly and respond in a timely fashion. Giving clients inaccurate information and then expecting them to accept anything else you say is not a workable scenario when doing home visits. Making it up as you go along—or worse, telling a client something you assume she wants to hear, regardless of accuracy, to move the visit along—will not make your job any easier in the long run.

Being an effective home visitor does not limit your communication exclusively to family child care providers. You must also be able to effectively communicate with your supervisor(s) about your concerns, observations, and any relevant feedback you receive from or about providers. In the case study that begins this module, Anna assures the client that she will communicate the client's feedback accurately and fairly. She has committed herself to actually doing just that when she returns to her office.

You often need to ask questions of your administrative staff when you are unsure of the information you are required to share. As an effective communicator, you need to be able to advocate for yourself as well as for your clients when you find it is necessary for you or them to obtain additional training or information.

CHECKPOINT—Your Role as Communicator

Before entering a provider's home, you should ask yourself the following questions:

- Do you fully understand the regulations and/or contractual information you are required to share with clients? Be honest with yourself. If there is information you are unsure about, get help. Ask questions and ask for examples if necessary. Do whatever it takes to feel confident that you understand the information you need to perform your job duties properly.

- Do you have ready access to training materials and to someone who can accurately answer your questions and/or to good written resources? If you do not have accessible and reliable resources, inform your supervisor. Get help in creating and organizing a resource file that will help you do your job more effectively.

- Do you feel you were given a sufficient opportunity to receive and process all the information necessary to do your job? Sometimes putting your best foot forward during an interview means you may have suggested that you know more than you actually do. Good subject knowledge is important, but visiting homes can be a challenging experience for anyone. Accompanying more experienced home visitors before going out on your own is always a good idea. Talk to your supervisor about this type of peer support.

- What would you like to see changed so you can better communicate necessary information? People will be unable to help you if they don't know you need assistance. Communicate your needs. Think about what would allow you to feel more confident when doing your job. Be specific.

The role of a communicator involves more than simply having a good understanding of the information you are obligated to share. Your level of confidence, your sincerity, your purposefulness, and your ability to empathize and find common goals and objectives are also important factors. Of all the characteristics that contribute to being a successful communicator, credibility is perhaps the most important. In establishing collaborative working arrangements, trust is a primary factor. Providers can't develop a trusting relationship with you if they do not believe what you say.

Quality Assurance Inspector

A story from Sharon: My first job was in a factory the summer before I started college. The work was hard. It was physically difficult as well as mentally stressful, because the machines I worked with did not always cooperate the way I needed them to. One afternoon my work area was visited by the quality assurance inspector. This person's job was to make sure the company was getting what it paid for. The inspector was there to observe the finished product as well as my effectiveness on the assembly line. To this day, I remember how unnerving that experience was to me.

Many years later, when I began visiting family child care homes, the feelings I'd experienced as a result of that quality assurance inspection came back to me. I remembered how nervous and uncomfortable I had been and as a result, how distrustful I had felt about the legitimacy of the process. Remembering those feelings helped me to strategize about what I could do to make my visits more effective without becoming confrontational or intimidating. I soon recognized that a small number of providers, no matter how I conducted my visits, would inevitably find any monitoring visits unpleasant experiences. That realization helped me to focus my attention on the large majority of programs in which I felt there was potential for successful and mutually beneficial visits. I quickly found that no one visit strategy worked with every client. I needed to employ specific visit strategies that corresponded to each client's personality and professional requirements. While an upbeat and energetic approach worked well with some clients, many others were more responsive to a slower, more studious approach. My experiences demonstrate that an important part of being an effective home visitor includes the ability to change tactics whenever necessary. It is also clear that the manner in which communication is delivered is often as important as the communication itself.

The role of quality assurance inspector is a big part of what you do. Because of the importance of your quality assurance responsibilities, this book includes other related modules: Maintain a Balance of Authority, Be Assertive, and Take Ethical Actions, for example. In this module, we focus on the interpersonal aspects of quality assurance and the importance of adequate physical and mental preparations for taking on this role.

You enter someone's home with the responsibility of determining whether or not that person is doing her job properly. Arguably, your profession requires you to police the business practices of the providers you visit. A negative observation may not only create uncomfortable feelings but could also result in the provider being denied reimbursement or suffering the loss of accreditation, her license, or children. In understanding your role as a quality assurance inspector, you must also understand how to fulfill that role by creating nonconfrontational visit strategies.

Strategies for Visits

One of the most effective strategies in promoting quality in the programs you visit is the creation of collaborative working relationships with your clients. Collaborative relationships always serve the quality assurance process in a positive way. If your clients have a clear understanding of your role and how it contributes to a positive outcome for both themselves and their children, your job becomes easier. Finding common goals is an effective way to demonstrate your willingness to assist a provider in operating a quality child care program.

While you are establishing appropriate professional boundaries, don't miss opportunities to create positive working relationships. Having appropriate professional boundaries and working collaboratively are not mutually exclusive concepts. Here's an example: As a home monitor for a food sponsor, you take the time to patiently teach a provider how to fill out a menu correctly. In doing so, you are demonstrating how this collaboration will benefit her and her program. When she receives her reimbursement in a timely fashion because she has submitted accurate menus, the benefits of your collaboration will be further reinforced. On the other hand, filling out a menu for a provider rather than teaching her to do so does not help you or your client. It may expedite your visit, but it does not empower the provider. Furthermore, it is not your responsibility. The large majority of providers want to do the job correctly. Providing good technical assistance in a patient, nonpatronizing way supports clients and allows them to feel they are capable of operating successful businesses.

In your role as a quality assurance inspector, one primary objective is to accurately determine the appropriateness of the services you monitor. Family child care providers are selling a service. In most instances, the organizations you represent are responsible for credentialing, monitoring, and/or reimbursing providers for all or some of those services. Consequently, a large part of your quality assurance role is to ensure that the service purchased or monitored by your organization is performed appropriately. How do you determine the appropriateness of a service?

Effective Evaluation

To determine the appropriateness of purchased or monitored services, you must understand exactly what the relevant service standards include. In cases involving reimbursement, you need to know the terms for reimbursement. If reimbursement is not involved, your role as quality assurance inspector may involve comparing the service provided to current compliance standards. This would be true in licensing or social service visits, for example. You need to know exactly what it is you should be observing and questioning during each visit. You may be expected to monitor all aspects of each child care program you visit. Components of child care may include, but are not limited to, enrollment, required record keeping, health and safety, abuse and neglect, physical environment, and age-appropriate curriculum and assessment.

If your organization has these expectations, you need to know and understand all the child care requirements in your state that pertain to family child care programs. These might include, for example, who is subject to a criminal background check or the ratio of enrolled children to provider. If you were not familiar with these requirements, you could not identify cases of illegal hiring or overenrollment.

Familiarizing yourself with basic requirements and regulations is also beneficial in creating collaborative working relationships. In many instances, clients will ask you for all types of information. If you are in a position to supply reliable information, your clients may come to see your visit as an asset rather than an intrusion.

Your experience, education, and good instincts are also very important in determining quality assurance. Keep in mind that it is natural for you to have personal opinions about what constitutes quality child care. Your opinions may have originated in your own childhood experiences or in experiences you had while raising your own children. You may have a standard you feel all child care providers should meet. Regardless of your opinions, you must recognize the fact that family child care comes in all shapes and sizes. While it is possible to hold personal opinions and still conduct objective and impartial assessments, this takes very conscious and planned effort on your part.

You should not assume anything. Your conclusions, when you make them, need to be based on what you have observed as well as on your total experience while in the provider's home. Do not come to conclusions about a provider's ability to care without being able to support those conclusions. If you conclude a provider is operating her business appropriately, remember you need to be able to support that assertion. The same holds true when your assessment is negative. As a quality assurance inspector, you are required to effectively support your conclusions with well-organized and understandable documentation.

Data Collection

In determining quality assurance, you need to use a reliable data collection instrument. Using a data collection tool that covers all the required points of information usually results in a more efficient visit. This tool should also help to ensure that no necessary topics are overlooked. For example, you may need to observe and monitor the components of a quality child care environment: accurate menus and appropriate meal preparation, safe physical environment, provider's ability to care for children, licensing and contract compliance, and stated curriculum and assessment objectives. In another case, you may arrive at the home to conduct an investigation or to collect specific follow-up information as a result of allegations made against a provider. Collecting information in an organized fashion allows you to maximize your available time and to create a relevant framework for your visit. As anyone who has visited a family child care home knows, there are generally more than enough distractions to go around. Your tools should allow you to stay focused.

Many home visitors work closely with or may actually work as licensers and social workers. Because of your official role, the information you collect during a home visit can have far-reaching ramifications. The better and more complete the tools you use for documenting what is observed, the easier your job will be, especially when and if it becomes necessary for you to communicate your observations to others. This is especially true if your documentation may be used as the basis for legal action.

For all of these reasons, your success as a quality assurance inspector depends on the careful design and use of data collection tools. Refine your tools based on your job requirements.

CHECKPOINT—Your Role as a Quality Assurance Inspector

Before entering a provider's home, ask yourself the following important questions:

- Do your clients believe you are fair and impartial when conducting your visits? If they do not, it's important to determine why. It is not enough simply to dismiss their opinions as a natural response to your role as a quality assurance inspector. Ask questions. Do not be afraid to solicit feedback from your clients. Demonstrate that constructive feedback can benefit both you and your clients.

- Are you prepared with materials on *current* technical assistance? There is no more effective way to conclude your visit than by leaving something helpful with the provider.

- Are you in the habit of finding at least one positive thing to say? If not, consider starting this practice. No matter what the situation, it's helpful to point out at least one positive. If you are looking at a cluttered environment, for example, you might introduce a positive comment about the amount of natural light before commenting on the clutter. When introducing a positive comment, remember that it should reflect something you actually observe. Providing balance in your feedback makes it easier for a client to accept a critical comment or evaluation.

- Have you ever made assumptions about the quality of care being provided based on the neighborhood or the outside appearance of the building where the care occurs? Never make assumptions about what is on the other side of the door. Make this your policy whether you are visiting in an inner-city neighborhood or an upscale suburb.

- Do you always provide written documentation to support your evaluations? If not, you need to start. Never leave yourself so vulnerable that you are unable to substantiate your conclusions. Do not try to depend solely on your memory. Eventually it will fail you. Document, document, document.

Public Relations Manager

Whether or not you choose to be, in countless ways you are the public face of your organization. Good public relations and good customer service generally go hand in hand. In many instances, your ability to do your job in a positive manner will make the difference in whether or not a provider affiliates with your organization or chooses to comply with a policy or regulation. Your public relations role is an important one.

Family child care can be a very isolating profession. Many providers see a home visit as a welcome opportunity to engage in conversation with another adult. When that welcome is offered to you, it presents a unique opportunity for a successful home visit experience. Sometimes a provider's isolation can make it more difficult to focus her attention on the business at hand. Some providers see a home visit as an opportunity to vent their frustration. Unfortunately, venting does not provide a lot of opportunity for conversation. Gossip also may be a favorite pastime for a provider eager for adult company and the opportunity to share what she considers news. This must be an absolute *no* for a home visitor—sharing personal information that is not relevant to the visit at hand is not appropriate. When you allow this type of conversation to occur, you permit your professional boundaries to be compromised, and you relinquish any authority you may have had going in. Your public relations role takes on special importance at moments like these.

Good public relations includes the ability to listen effectively while someone expresses feelings while still being able to bring the conversation back to the point. This ability is essential for home visits to be productive. You may also find it necessary, in a polite but firm manner, to redirect the conversation when it begins to move into areas that are not relevant and that may compromise confidentiality. Good public relations include organizing successful visits that assist you and the provider in maintaining your respective roles. A client should not discuss her own or another provider's marital problems, for example, if this information is not relevant to child care. As an effective public relations person, remember: You are a resource, not a confidante.

Simply making the visit should not and cannot be your primary objective. Planning your agenda and specific objectives before conducting your visit helps you exercise the control necessary to subtly direct subject matter and focus. Doing this in positive and organized ways allows you to present a good public relations persona for yourself as well as your organization. A provider exposed to good public relations has had behavior modeled for her that she can then use in the operation of her own business, especially when dealing with parents.

Good Public Relations Goals

In your role as public relations manager, you can consistently work toward fulfilling key goals. Not surprisingly, these goals along with the objectives you have established in your other roles as a home visitor often overlap. These general public relations goals include the following:

- Establishing realistic expectations for each home visit
- Presenting accurate information and assessments fairly and consistently
- Employing tools that allow you to maximize the time spent during your visit
- Thoroughly understanding any information it is your job to convey
- Being prepared to write down any questions you are unable to answer and having the appropriate resources to respond to them accurately and in a timely fashion
- Being on time for and being timely during the visit
- Treating a family child care provider, her home, her family, and all the children present with respect
- Receiving the respect and attention of the people you visit
- Successfully identifying and communicating the benefits of compliance as part of a working collaboration between you and your client

The Importance of Consistency

Consistency is an important aspect of good public relations. The way in which you conduct a home visit should be predictable. That does not mean every home visit will be the same. It does mean that your presentation—including your appearance, voice, and body language—should remain consistent, even if the client's does not. It also means that your ability to remain objective, calm, and impartial should be consistent during each visit. If a client becomes agitated over something discussed during a home visit, for example, your response needs to be consistently calm and moderate.

Striking the Right Tone

In some instances, clients will stay affiliated with your organization because of the personal relationships they believe they have established with you. This may occasionally create a dilemma for you. It always feels good when the people you work with like you. Nonetheless, you must remember that you are visiting a client's home for professional, not personal, reasons. You need to be able to accomplish your objectives whether or not you are liked. A client does not have to like you personally in order to respect and welcome the assistance you can provide. A good approach many successful professionals employ is to establish a working connection based solely on the professional services you are in the home to provide. This means that your emphasis during a home visit should consistently be about the duties you are there to perform. For example, you may sit on a town board. Your client may have questions that deal with your town board responsibilities. It would be preferable for you to refer her to another board member. Confining your conversation to the visit and avoiding subjects such as the softball league that both your children participate in is another example of keeping your relationship professional. The benefit of maintaining professionalism is threefold:

1. You can introduce constructive or critical feedback, when necessary, without the client interpreting your observations as a personal betrayal.
2. Other individuals with similar job responsibilities can conduct home visits with your client without difficulty.
3. Clients can observe your professional behavior and perhaps replicate it with their own clients.

Good public relations involve positive energy and good preplanning on your part. Staying current and well informed is certainly important. Self-assessment is a big part of being an effective public relations manager and offering good customer service.

 CHECKPOINT—Your Role as a Public Relations Manager

Before entering a client's home, ask yourself the following important questions:

• Do you remain current? Are your resources up to date, and do you ask appropriate questions when you are unsure of policies and procedures? You cannot adequately represent your organization in your public relations role without knowing what you are doing and saying. Many providers are understandably dissatisfied at feeling they know a whole lot more about your work than you do. If a client feels she has to teach you your job, you are definitely in trouble.

- Are you adversarial? Are there some clients who simply rub you the wrong way based on personality or a negative visit experience? Does your voice or confrontational stance mirror that of the provider when she is angry or upset? Adversarial behavior has no place during a home visit. There is no positive outcome for you or the client. You also contribute to a tense and stressful situation for the children in care. Don't ever be afraid to end a visit if you feel things are getting out of control. You can also suggest taking a break for a moment so you can both regain your composure. You are not going to win a screaming match, and it is totally inappropriate of you to try. You are not backing down if you maintain a calm composure or elect to end a visit. Go back to your office, discuss what occurred with your supervisor, and regroup.

- Do you have a me-versus-them attitude? Does this attitude surface when you enter a client's home for a monitoring visit? Although you are there to monitor and evaluate, you aren't doing yourself or your client any favors when she can justifiably assume you are there solely to catch her doing something wrong. That does not motivate a client to do her best, and it is certainly not the message you want to convey. You may in fact ultimately identify things she is doing incorrectly, but there should always be the understanding that you are in a home to objectively collect information. If the goal is ultimately what is best for children while in child care, that goal should be shared by everyone involved. In that respect, remember that you and the client are both on the same team.

- Do you truly listen to what clients say, or are you so caught up in your own sense of authority that you are unwilling to actually hear what is being said? In thinking about what made me most uncomfortable during that quality assurance inspection in the factory many years ago, I eventually recognized it was the fact that the inspector never once looked me in the eye. She wrote on her clipboard almost without looking up at all. My personal value during that inspection seemed limited to how many pocket patches I could pack. The providers you visit deserve better. Whether your overall assessment is positive or negative, you rarely create positive results by dehumanizing the experience. Take the time while taking notes or filling out data collection sheets to stop and listen while looking your client in the eye.

Role Model

One of the most frequently repeated adages about children in early child care is "They learn from what they see and do rather than from what they hear an adult say." The accuracy of this axiom is not limited to young children. If we are all honest with ourselves, we will readily admit we generally remember less than half of what we are told. We retain only a portion of what we read. More often than not, we believe what we see. This is the information we are most likely to retain.

When you enter a family child care provider's home, you should be setting the stage for a positive learning experience. One of the ways you do this is by presenting yourself as an appropriate role model.

Appearance

Never underestimate the power of your appearance. Family child care providers, in part because their work is home based and their daily interactions are usually limited to small children, can sometimes neglect their own appearance. Many providers fall into patterns that adversely affect their ability to maintain full enrollment or attract new clients. Nothing, for example, irritates parents more than dropping off their child to a provider still dressed in her pajamas. Your visit to a family child care home presents a great opportunity to model professional appearance.

Your dress should reflect your professionalism. In dressing appropriately, you demonstrate that you understand you're not simply visiting the client's home but also their place of business. A client will be instantly aware of your overall appearance, even if she does not comment on it. If you look like a mess when you visit, do not be surprised if the visit does not go as well as you originally planned. Your appearance as a home visitor in many ways demonstrates the degree of respect you have for a provider, her business, and her home. If she suspects your appearance demonstrates a lack of respect or a lack of professionalism, she may respond in a disrespectful and unprofessional manner.

An important part of planning a successful home visit, then, is to dress appropriately. Professional dress should err on the side of conservatism. The following guidelines are recommended when you are deciding what to wear during work hours.

Women	Men
Skirts should be knee-length or longer so you can sit gracefully.	Wear clean pants that fit conservatively and do not have holes or tears.
Pants and shirts should be comfortable, not too tight, without holes or elaborate decorations. Their fit should avoid exposing your midriff.	Wear neatly pressed shirts. Long or short sleeves are fine. Buttoned shirts should be closed up to the top one or two buttons.
Stick to comfortable, closed-toe shoes.	Choose comfortable, closed-toe shoes.
Avoid heavy makeup and extremely long fingernails.	Avoid looking unkempt and displaying unusual piercings.
Wear minimal jewelry or piercings.	Bring a professional bag to hold all the necessary materials you will need for your visit.
Bring a professional bag to hold all the necessary materials you will need for your visit.	Avoid strong fragrances. Wear deodorant or antiperspirant. Think clean. You need to look pulled together during your visit. You should have clean nails, clean skin, dry, neatly arranged hair, and practice good dental hygiene.
Avoid strong fragrances. Wear deodorant or antiperspirant. Think clean. You need to look pulled together during your visit. You should have clean nails, clean skin, dry, neatly arranged hair, and practice good dental hygiene.	

While you need to look neat and professional for your visit, you should also dress for comfort, confidence, and safety. Seasons play a role in how you dress. The shoes you wear in summer, for example, will be different from those you may need in winter. In summary, it is important to remember that your appearance should not become a distraction or a focal point during a professional visit.

Confidentiality

A home visitor should never engage in gossip or breach confidentiality. This was discussed in connection with your public relations manager role. It is worth repeating here because it's such an important part of your function as a role model. If a client attempts to share private and/or embarrassing information, that is not relevant, about herself, another provider, or a child care family member, you need to end the conversation. As a home visitor, your responsibility is to focus the discussion on the actual purpose of the visit. If the provider is concerned about the health and safety of any child and has concerns regarding abuse or neglect, in those instances your ability to respond appropriately is important. Having information on hand that outlines the provider's responsibility as well as procedures for reporting abuse is extremely helpful. In most states, licensed providers have regulatory and legal responsibilities as mandated reporters.

Many providers find themselves in vulnerable positions because they have not successfully established professional boundaries with the parents of children enrolled in their programs. Your ability to demonstrate courteous and appropriate behaviors while accomplishing the objectives of your visit may assist providers in creating their own professional boundaries and practicing confidentiality. When you and a client share inappropriate information that is not relevant to the home visit or the safety of enrolled children, it is not so much a sign of collaborative success as a sign of dysfunction.

In some instances, a client may break confidentiality to distract you from the actual purpose of your home visit. Getting off track by telling stories that are not related to the visit is a common avoidance strategy of people who are uncomfortable. If this happens frequently when you visit a provider, you should think about why it's happening and what you can do to prevent this from occurring. You might ask yourself these questions:

- How quickly do you get to the point? Might the provider be replicating your style?
- Are you facilitating these getting-off-the-track strategies because you are uncomfortable about confronting specific issues?
- Do you arrive at a client's home with absolutely no visit plan and essentially leave the pace and focus of the visit to the client?

Value of Feedback

As a home visitor, you need to reinforce the understanding that you are in a provider's home for professional reasons. You are visiting, but you are visiting with a purpose. That said, a home visit should not be so structured as to be rigid. You should never be unfriendly, and the visit should not be unduly stressful for you or your client. None of those characteristics are synonymous with professionalism.

Occasionally a client may talk incessantly because she is nervous. It's important to ask yourself what components of your visit may be creating tension for the provider. Ask yourself if there are ways for you to reduce that tension. Ask the provider if there is something under your control that you can do differently to enhance the visit. In doing this, you are demonstrating that feedback can benefit you as well as your client. Soliciting feedback to improve the visit experience also provides your client with a good example for her future provider-parent interactions.

Understanding the Environment

Remember that providers are busy caring for children. The more you demonstrate that you have a purpose and that you can conduct your business in a timely fashion, the more effectively you model efficient organization of time.

On occasion, it is not the provider who creates a distraction but the children. Children invariably sense when their caregiver is uncomfortable or stressed. Often this can trigger chaotic and inappropriate behavior. Sometimes a provider clearly demonstrates she does not have adequate control over her child care environment. In such cases, children's disruptive behavior often is the obvious result. It's important for you to be sensitive to the environment when you're conducting your home visits.

Usually, if a provider understands your role and feels confident that your assessment will be fair and straightforward, tension should be minimal. In most cases, if you are using your public relations and quality assurance skills appropriately, over time clients will recognize the collaborative benefit of your visits. When providers begin to feel comfortable with you, the children in their programs will also welcome your arrival. Sometimes getting to this point requires lots of patience and good planning on your part. Don't ignore what you see, but rather use it as an opportunity. Suggesting quiet activities for children during your visit may be helpful. If a provider appears to offer little or no schedule of activities that could give her some control over her child care group, you can offer her technical assistance. Your ability to offer focused help provides you with yet another opportunity to create a collaborative working relationship while modeling effective strategies.

Many home visitors interact with the children in the client's program. This provides a great opportunity for you to demonstrate positive behaviors. For example, when you speak softly and calmly to children, you are demonstrating an appropriate behavior—not only to the children, but also to the provider. If during a visit you observe a provider whose tone or body language is less than nurturing, take advantage of your visit to model more nurturing behavior. This will demonstrate an alternative approach.

A story from Sharon: I can recall one provider who was loving and experienced, but she had a gruff voice. When children were first enrolled in her program, many of them appeared frightened. This perplexed me. I recognized the provider's many strengths, but I felt uncomfortable seeing new children appear so unhappy. When I raised the issue of newly enrolled children and how I felt they responded to her, she laughed it off. She said, "The children will get accustomed to me eventually." So whenever I entered that home, I made it part of my visit strategy to sit and talk quietly, especially with new children. I worked very hard at demonstrating behaviors I felt would help make new children feel safe and comfortable. Eventually, not because of anything I said to her but because of how she saw me interact with the children, I began to see her make more attempts at allowing new children to see the softer side of her personality. Truly, your ability to model appropriate behavior cannot be underestimated.

Organization

A home visitor should find it difficult to comment on a provider's organizational skills if the home visitor herself demonstrates no sense of organization during a visit. Your position as a role model is never so apparent as when you are demonstrating good organizational skills. It's important that you are prepared to conduct a well-organized and efficient visit as soon as you arrive. For example, if you are constantly running out to your car to grab something you have forgotten, think about the message that sends to your client. You are essentially saying the visit is not very important to you—certainly not important enough for you to come prepared. You are also sending the message that disorganization is really no big deal. Yet in many instances, organization—or lack of it—will be a key factor in your client's ability to operate a successful business. Consequently, disorganization is not a behavior you should model for your child care clients.

Modeling good organizational skills helps you shape professional visits and ultimately benefits your client as well as yourself. Plan your visit before arriving at the family child care home. If, for example, you have observed that a provider lacks understanding of appropriate food storage or behavior guidance strategies, arriving at her home with resource materials that target these specific areas of assistance reflects good visit planning. You are offering your client useful and needed information that will improve the quality of her program. You are also demonstrating how this home visit warranted preparation on your part. Because good preparation is essential in operating a well-run child care program, modeling this behavior helps your client understand her obligation to also plan ahead and prepare accordingly.

Demonstrating good organizational skills during a visit includes bringing the materials necessary for the visit. You should not be borrowing pens or paper from a provider because you do not have them with you. We are all human, and it is not unheard of to forget something you need. Such an occasion should be the exception rather than the rule. Preparation for a visit should include listing what you hope to accomplish as well as what you want to share with your client. If resource or training material is part of your visit plan, make sure you have included it.

When scheduling a visit, you should allocate the amount of time you will need based on what you will be doing during that visit. Providers appreciate knowing approximately how long you will be in their homes. Thinking about your visit and planning your agenda before you arrive will allow you to schedule effectively and demonstrate the benefits that can result from good organization.

Arriving on time is another example of good organization. If you consistently arrive much later or much earlier than you originally arranged with your client, you are not modeling appropriate behavior; instead, you are reinforcing the idea that her time and profession are simply not as important as yours. Your position as a monitor or evaluator of child care settings does not make your profession more important than the provider's. When examining your responsibility as a role model, remember how many important roles family child care providers play. If you are in the habit of conducting unannounced visits, remember to inform your client of this when you first meet with her.

Your obligation to provide appropriate role modeling is all-inclusive. For example, if you are a smoker, you should not sit in your car in full view of a provider and her enrolled children to have a cigarette before you make your visit. Your language should be tailored to the environment you are visiting: never use rude language in the presence of providers and children. Modeling good behavior does not mean you need to submerge your personality and become robotic. It does mean that you must have a heightened awareness of your environment and how to affect it positively. Behaviors you want to see repeated need to be reinforced. One of the most effective ways of reinforcing positive behaviors is to demonstrate them repeatedly.

CHECKPOINT—The Role of Role Model

Before entering a provider's home, ask yourself the following questions—they will help you employ a proactive approach in developing your daily visit routines:

- Do you plan ahead and wear specific clothing for work, or do you grab whatever is available in the morning? We can tell you from personal experience that providers who may not appear to notice what you are wearing during your visit are not the least bit reluctant to talk about you once you have left. Never underestimate the importance of your appearance when you are conducting business. People do notice, and they respond accordingly.

- How organized are you during your visits? If you are in the habit of forgetting many things and are constantly promising that you will remember to bring something the next time, you are not doing yourself any favors. Eventually, providers will catch on that you will conduct the next visit in a manner no more efficient than the preceding visit. Once you have lost the professional respect of the people you monitor, your job becomes that much more difficult. Be on top of your visit, and never promise to bring something the next time and then not do it.

This module identifies the many roles played by the home visitor. You can probably think of many more—teacher, advocate, adviser are only a few that readily come to mind. As you embrace each role that describes your specific job, remember to identify the skill set that will help you do that job well.

CHECKPOINT—Putting the Roles Together

You need information to do your job effectively. Before scheduling your home visits, carefully review the following information.
    You should know the following:

- ☐ Current regulations and contractual information

- ☐ Where to get accurate information in a timely fashion if you cannot answer a question immediately

☐ Sufficient information about each program to create effective and personalized visiting strategies

☐ How to conduct visits in a professional manner

☐ How to objectively observe and document what occurs during a visit and how to create fair and impartial assessments

☐ What to wear and, more important, what not to wear

☐ How and when to model behaviors to help providers enhance their child care programs

Use Your Senses

Module Description

This module identifies the types of information you can gather through each of your senses during home visits. The information contained demonstrates how using your senses effectively enhances your ability to do your job. In this module, what you should and shouldn't see, hear, and smell in a child care setting is discussed in a candid and relevant manner. This module also addresses how your instincts, based on the information received from your senses, can be used to assist you in providing objective and factual evaluations.

Learning Objectives

- Employ your senses in a way that assists you while you are monitoring homes.
- Know the importance of identifying the origin of unusual smells or noises.
- Use information you gather from all your senses when creating assessments.
- Trust and understand your senses as they apply to your job.
- Listen to that little voice inside your head when it tells you things are not quite right.
- Use information collected through your senses to support your conclusions when you are documenting the events that occurred during a home visit.

· · · · · · · · ·

Case Study

· ·

Karen, a home visitor, has just completed an especially difficult visit. The provider's home was chaotic and unsanitary. The situation in this home had deteriorated a great deal since Karen's last visit. When Karen returns to her office, she sits down to document her assessment. She thinks it will be easy to write her report because the experience is still so vivid in her mind.

As Karen sits at her desk writing, her supervisor peeks over her shoulder. Karen explains she is about to send the supervisor her report about an awful home visit. As her supervisor reads the report, she stops and tells Karen that simply saying the visit was awful and the home was unsanitary is insufficient. It is important that in the body of the report Karen explain how she reached those conclusions.

Karen thinks for a moment and begins to organize her ideas. First, she attempts to identify why she characterized this program as chaotic. She develops the following list:

- As I approached the front door, I could hear the sound of the provider and the children screaming at one another.
- When I entered the home, I heard the television at what sounded to be full volume, as well as the noise of children running from room to room, shouting at the provider and one another. I could also hear the provider yelling, attempting to be heard over the noise.
- While I heard all of these things, I could also see the clutter and debris in the rooms used by the children. Toys and materials were strewn about, almost as if the children's last activity had been to see how many objects they could throw on the floor.
- I could also see younger children attempting to find places to hide so they would not be knocked over by the older children running about the house.
- Upon entering the provider's home, I could smell a strong musty odor. When I attempted to identify its origin, I found nap mats piled high in the front foyer. The odor was coming from these unwashed nap mats.
- When I entered the kitchen, I immediately smelled garbage. I became aware as I followed my nose that the provider had not

emptied the trash container. It sat accessible to children in the kitchen area, overflowing and uncovered.

- When I entered the playroom, I could smell the fish tank. It was obvious that the tank had not been cleaned for a long period, and the odor was very strong.
- I was able to see crumbs on the kitchen table and floor, neither of which had been wiped down or swept.
- I could also see children with unwashed hands and faces.

As Karen reworks her report, she integrates all of the information she received by using her senses. In writing her conclusion, she uses the evidence she gathered from her eyes, nose, and ears to support it. After reading Karen's final report, her supervisor has no problem forming an image of the condition of this home.

. . . .

What You Smell

The sense of smell is primitive as well as powerful. Frequently, when you are attempting to assess whether or not an environment is sanitary, your sense of smell becomes an important ally. On occasion, your sense of smell can alert you to issues you may be unable to see when you first enter a family child care home.

We are usually able to notice new odors immediately. Within a few minutes after exposure, however, we are often no longer able to smell even the strongest odors as acutely. This may create a problem when you are attempting to identify an odor's source. When odors are an issue, it is a good idea to find a reason to go outside at some point during your visit. You may use the opportunity to observe an outside play area, for example. This break should allow you to be more successful in determining the source of any unpleasant odors when you return inside.

It is never easy to tell a provider her home has an unpleasant smell. This is an area of discussion that is often uncomfortable for both the home visitor and the client. As a result, it is usually more helpful to focus on the source of the unpleasant odor than on the odor itself. For example, it is easier to ask a provider politely if she has had an opportunity to dispose of her trash than to simply say, "Your house smells bad."

You can also remind providers that prospective parents get their initial and most powerful impressions when they enter a child care program for the first time. Providers should not want a prospective family's first impression to be based on unsanitary and powerful odors. Child care environments should smell like the good things happening within them: healthy food; flowers and greenery; paints, crayons, clay, and other materials that may be used in the home. Smells send powerful signals to children and their families. The following are potential problems that may be identified by your sense of smell.

Pets

Many providers include pets as part of their child care curriculum. Some providers simply allow their own household pets to be in the same areas of the home they use for child care. Your feedback to a provider on this issue is important. For example, if the dog smells bad, the provider may not realize it. Because the dog is hers, she may have lost her ability to smell an odor that has been present for a while. In these instances, you need to be able to say, "The dog smells bad." Any animal that gives off a strong odor may not be well and could pose a health hazard to children in care. Fish tanks, bird cages, containers that house gerbils or hamsters—all can be sources of odors. A provider needs to know that the ultimate responsibility for taking care of a pet cannot fall solely on a child, either a child in care or her own child. Ultimately, it is the provider's responsibility to care for pets and ensure a clean environment.

LITTER BOXES

Regardless of whether or not children have direct access to a cat litter box, if you can smell the box when you enter the home, a health issue exists. Regardless of whether the provider's cat and the litter box are located in a separate or unlicensed part of the child care home, if you can smell the litter box in the child care area, a problem exists that needs to be corrected immediately.

Diaper and Toilet Odors

If you smell urine and/or feces, your first question might be, "Where and how frequently do you dispose of diapers?" This type of odor should tell you immediately that the disposal procedure for diapers may be inadequate or that the trash container is not appropriately covered and positioned. Regulatory requirements dealing with placement of trash containers and the necessity for covers that fit appropriately are common. Make sure you have ready access to this information when applicable, and make it available to the provider during your visit. Another source of odor may be children whose diapers are not being changed often enough. If this is the case, you need to address this with the provider immediately.

Garbage

Other strong and unpleasant odors that originate in trash containers may have nothing to do with dirty diapers. If you can smell the trash upon entering a home, this problem needs to be addressed immediately.

Mold and Mildew

Many providers find using their basement a great way to separate the space allocated for child care from the other parts of their home. That's all well and good as long as the basement is properly ventilated, has sufficient light and appropriate exits, and does not contain mold or mildew. Mold and mildew can contribute to illness in children and in some cases result in allergic reactions. If you enter any room in a provider's home and smell mold or mildew, tell the provider. A family child care provider needs to know this can pose potential health hazards that need to be dealt with as quickly as possible.

Disinfectants and Harsh Cleansers

Many disinfectants and cleansers contain harmful chemicals, such as ammonia, petrochemicals, and volatile organic compounds (VOCs). It is risky for providers to have these products in their homes because of the potential for accidental ingestion or physical contact. If providers use these types of disinfectants, they need to demonstrate how they make them inaccessible to children. In addition, breathing the fumes of some chemicals like chlorine bleach, especially over time, can be damaging to health. If providers are using bleach as a disinfectant and they are using it appropriately, you should not be able to smell chlorine when you enter the home. If you can smell chlorine, talk with the provider about the amount and mixture of bleach solution she is using to disinfect. Small amounts of residual product may linger on surfaces or in the air following cleaning and disinfecting, adversely affecting the home's air quality. Some providers assume that because they can smell disinfectant, their homes are germ free. It's important to communicate the fact that being able to smell a disinfectant is simply not healthy.

Alcohol, Drugs, and Smoking

If your sense of smell tells you that possible problems with alcohol or drugs exist, you should document what you smell and discuss your impressions with a supervisor. Smoking in close proximity to children is also a health risk you can often identify, using your sense of smell. If you can smell cigarette smoke when you enter a family child care home, it is important to talk with the provider about this. Most states prohibit smoking in the presence of children in child care. If you can smell cigarettes on a provider's clothes and breath or on the clothes of participating children, it is necessary to ask how she is accommodating her smoking habit while providing for the health and safety of the children enrolled in her program. Make providers aware of the danger of smoking in the presence of children. Always provide your client with all of the resource materials you have available to you about the health and safety of children to reinforce your message.

In summary, don't be afraid that you are more sensitive to odors than you should be. If you can smell an unpleasant odor in a child care setting, no matter how subtle, it constitutes a potential health risk as well as a probable maintenance problem. As strange as it may sound, if your goal is to create collaborative working relationships with the providers you monitor, you must be straightforward about bad odors. Most providers will recognize that although hearing this type of feedback is not always comfortable, receiving it from you is preferable to a parent removing a child from the program because of unpleasant odors.

You should not ignore your sense of smell. It may be tempting to ignore what cannot be seen, especially because bringing it up can be uncomfortable or embarrassing. But if you can smell an unhealthy or unpleasant odor, ask what it is and where the odor is coming from. Make sure you include in your documentation what you smelled and where you smelled it.

 CHECKPOINT—Your Sense of Smell

When entering a home, you should ask the following questions if there are unpleasant odors:

- Is there appropriate ventilation?

- Are there appropriate procedures for disposing of garbage?

- Do you check to see which rooms unpleasant odors come from?

- Are you able to effectively confront a provider when you become aware of an unhealthy odor?

- Do you offer resource materials to providers about odors that adversely affect health and safety?

What You Hear

Being aware of the regularity, volume, and sources of sounds within a family child care home is very important. Loud or prolonged noise often tires people, especially young children. Trying to concentrate through noise is very difficult for the provider and the children. Noise distracts and makes it harder for young children to pay attention and to learn. Noise often gets in the way of good communication and can lead to errors and misunderstandings. Noise interferes with warm, caring relationships, because noise prevents providers from being able to speak softly to children and speaking softly communicates closeness. Noise can permanently damage hearing. Noise can also make it very difficult for children with any degree of hearing impairment to function. Ideally, what a home visitor should hear in a child care setting is the happy, busy hum of children who are involved in activities they enjoy.

When using your sense of hearing during a visit, you may find the following information helpful.

Indoor Volume

If you need to raise your voice substantially to be heard, you should determine why.

TELEVISION

If the majority of loud sound is coming from the television when you arrive, observe closely. How are the children occupied at the time of your visit? Question the provider about the volume of the television, and ask how frequently it is on. The provider may suggest to you that the only reason the children are watching television is to allow her to focus some attention on your visit. You can offer alternative suggestions to television, such as books and puzzles. Having resource materials available about the use of television in child care would also be helpful. At the very least, the television should be adjusted so the volume is not overpowering.

CHILDREN

Are the children behaving in a manner that is loud and chaotic? Home visitors know it is not unusual in a child care environment for children to act out at the arrival of a new person. There is a distinct difference, however, between children who are momentarily disruptive and children who are out of control from the time you enter the front door until the time you leave. If the setting is unduly loud and chaotic, it is appropriate to bring this to the attention of the provider. An effective strategy might be giving the provider technical assistance targeted at scheduling activities or guiding behaviors. You may be surprised at how many providers feel overwhelmed and will jump at the offer to obtain some assistance.

Listening to the way children address one another can be very revealing. Is the tone positive? Listen to the children when you visit a family child care home. How do they speak to one another? Children will tease and sometimes tattle on other children when an adult enters their child care setting; this should usually be in the form of good-natured bantering. Small children collectively are usually not bad tempered and negative. When listening to the children in the program, ask yourself if their tone and body language reflect the tone and body language of the provider.

Provider's Voice

What tone of voice does the provider usually use during your visit? Are the provider and the children screaming to be heard? Some providers are in the habit of speaking loudly to gain the attention of the children. These providers may become oblivious to the tone of their voice or the volume of sound in their home. Often a provider does not realize that her voice has doubled in volume when she speaks to children. You have a great opportunity to model appropriate communication. Always speak in a soft, calm voice. Often when you speak softly, you will note an almost immediate mirrored response from the provider and children.

Does the provider's tone change when she is talking to you? A story from Sharon: I frequently had the experience of visiting a home in which the provider could not have been sweeter or used a more pleasing tone of voice than when she and I were speaking. Yet in the next moment, she would turn and yell at a child who may have inadvertently interrupted her. This type of Jekyll and Hyde behavior is not comfortable to observe. An effective strategy that often works is to immediately address the children in a soft and calm voice. Most astute providers will pick up on the fact that your communication style differs greatly from theirs. For those who do not seem to get the message, make behavioral guidance resource materials available. When you distribute the materials, let providers know you are sharing this type of resource based on the communication you heard between the provider and children in care.

Listen to how the provider speaks to children. Do you ever hear menacing or demeaning words? A story from Sharon: I once visited a family child care for the purpose of renewing its license. At the time of my visit, the provider was offering foster care in conjunction with family child care. Two foster children were present, a little boy and a little girl. The provider proceeded to tell me about her intention to adopt the little girl and about how much her family loved this child. In the next instant, the provider pointed to the little boy, who was approximately four years old, and began to tell me he was a "terrible child" and she "could not wait to get rid of him." As long as I live, I will never forget the look of hurt in that child's eyes. If a provider is sharing information with you that is demeaning to a child in the presence of that child, that child care setting has a problem. If the provider I described above spoke about the little boy in that manner when I was present, what was she saying to him when I was not there?

Household Members

Are there household members present during the visit, and if so, how are they contributing to the volume of sound in the child care area? A provider's own children are often the most likely to become disruptive during a home visit. In many instances, such behavior is their way of telling you this is their home, and "don't make the mistake of confusing me with a child care child." Offer the provider resource material that speaks to this issue. Sometimes another adult is present in the home and attempts to discipline children supposedly in order for the provider to focus on your visit. If the interaction between the household member and the children is loud, intimidating, or in any other way inappropriate, you should bring this to the attention of the child care provider immediately. Remember, whatever the circumstances, you should consistently maintain a moderate tone and volume when speaking.

Sound Absorption

Soft items, such as throw pillows and rugs, can soften the volume of sound in the child care environment. If you walk into a setting in which every sound is amplified, make helpful suggestions. A provider may not realize that her program is unusually loud, especially if it is the only child care setting she has seen. Your ability to give accurate feedback as well as to provide reliable resources will be a valuable asset to her. This will also reinforce the collaborative working relationship you are trying to establish.

Absence of Sounds

An unruly, noisy environment is cause for concern, but so is the absence of sound in a rigid or overly structured program. In a quality child care environment, you should be able to hear the sounds of children throughout your visit. The sounds of childhood can sometimes be loud, but even loud sounds should be productive and delightful. If you are listening carefully, what you hear when entering a child care environment can help you conduct an effective home visit.

Identifying Sources of Sounds

Listen for children you can't see. A story from Sharon: I occasionally had the experience when doing home visits of hearing children in other areas of the home. In most instances, the children were the provider's own children, who were playing outside the area designated for child care. However, in some instances the children I heard were children who had been purposefully removed from the child care area so I would not know the provider was overenrolled. On one occasion, I actually heard an infant crying outside the child care area. After much discussion, the provider admitted to hiding the infant in an upstairs bathroom with the clothes dryer running so I would not be able to hear the infant if she cried. Fortunately, I was listening.

. . . .

Listening in a family child care environment is not always easy. A lot is usually going on, and it can be distracting. But the ability to be a good listener is especially important when you are monitoring a child care setting. What you hear can sometimes be different from what you see. That is when your ability to listen becomes most valuable. Remember when you are documenting your visit to include conclusions based not solely on what you saw but also on what you heard.

 CHECKPOINT—Your Sense of Hearing

During a home visit, ask yourself the following questions:

- Do you check the level of sound when you enter the child care setting?

- Do you observe whether the television is on and at what volume?

- Do you listen to the tone of the provider, household members, and participating children?

- Do you hear something that contradicts what you have been told or what you see?

- Are you prepared to give technical assistance about softening the volume of sound in the environment?

What You See

What you see when you enter a family child care setting tells you a great deal about the program. You should see evidence of appropriate services and activities. Challenge yourself on occasion to enter a home and try to see it as if this were your first visit. Sometimes what you expect to see unduly influences what you actually do see.

Things You Should See

You should expect to see certain things in a child care environment. If they are missing, look more closely for related problems.

A CLUTTER-FREE APPEARANCE

The setting should offer ample room for children and adults to move about freely. When people cannot move about easily, they are at risk for injuries. In addition, physical development should be an important objective in a provider's early child care curriculum. Children need room to grow and develop in healthy ways. If the environment appears too crowded, ask how healthy physical development is accomplished.

Some clutter is normal in a child care environment. However, it should not pose a hazard or risk, and it should not be so extensive that children cannot productively engage in activities. Good clutter is usually the result of children's normal activities. Bad clutter, on the other hand, very often consists of debris, broken toys, too many materials, and too little storage.

SPACES THAT SUPPORT SOCIAL INTERACTIONS

Space arrangements should reflect an understanding of how children interact. Everyone needs spaces that encourage interactions with others. Equally important, spaces should allow for private time. Think about the difference between homes and institutional settings. Homes should have spaces for different activities. Encourage the provider to be creative and to take full advantage of her home. Unused nooks, crannies, and corners in many homes can offer small children spaces in which to read quietly or work on a puzzle. These are sometimes overlooked by providers. Your technical assistance can be invaluable in helping your clients use their space effectively.

PERSONALIZATION

The family child care home should reflect the tastes and interests of the children it serves. The environment should be arranged to reflect the individual needs of the children in care. For example, the home should incorporate and emphasize children's artwork, crafts, and photographs of people and places that are meaningful to the children. Space for enrolled infants should be identifiable.

A family child care environment often serves as a family's living area as well as a provider's business, and you should be able to observe indications that both functions are adequately provided for. A family child care home should look like a home. At the same time, anyone entering the home should be able to immediately identify this as a setting that includes the care of children.

GENERAL ORDERLINESS

The child care environment should seem organized but not rigidly so. Convenient and sufficient storage space should keep activity supplies and equipment out of the way when they are not in use. The purpose of all child care is to promote and support self-reliance, so the environment should not be organized in a way that makes children unnecessarily dependent on the provider. Children should be able to initiate activities and be encouraged to put things away after they are finished. When a setting looks compulsively clean and nothing is out of place, you should suspect that children cannot behave naturally.

NORMAL SOCIALIZATION

Look at the way the provider and children interact. Caring providers should be listening and talking to children, responding to their needs, and occasionally using friendly touches to communicate their interest and affection. Children, for the most part, should be playing and talking with one another. The provider should be circulating and skillfully helping children to establish or succeed in their socializing or their activities. A skillful provider helps without taking over or unduly directing children. She should redirect or avert risky or unacceptable behavior without making a big issue of it. Everyone—providers, children, any household members who are present—should appear comfortable interacting with one other.

CHILDREN'S ACTIVE INVOLVEMENT

A home visitor needs to look at how involved or engaged children are in their activities and with one another. If they are tuned out, they may be staring into space, perhaps whining, or otherwise trying to escape the situation. If the provider is not trying to engage the children or is criticizing them for being uninvolved, a problem is likely. A skillful provider promotes natural social involvement and can usually keep everyone engaged in activities that interest them.

INVOLVEMENT OF HOUSEHOLD MEMBERS

In a family child care home, household members are important parts of the social environment. How do they interact with the provider and with children who are present? Do they identify children by name, for example?

QUALITY CARE

It is simply not true that intangible things like affection, concern, care, or quality cannot be observed. On occasion a provider will show you only what she wants you to see. If you are responsible for monitoring the child care environment, you must take charge of the visit. Remember your role as quality assurance inspector. (See module 1.)

Things You Should Not See

Along with things you should be looking for in a child care environment, you should also be on the lookout for things you should never see. Here are some common problems.

OVERENROLLMENT

Overenrollment is a serious problem. Adequately supervising large numbers of children while providing the care and attention each child needs is a challenging task. Providers who care for more children than the number specified on their license are not only compromising their ability to maintain their license; they are also potentially endangering the children in their program. If you are monitoring, count heads. Know how many children the provider is licensed to care for at any one time.

UNSUPERVISED CHILDREN

Children enrolled in child care programs should be supervised. Most states have regulatory language that speaks to this issue. Children should not be on different floors than the provider. Children should not be in closed rooms where providers cannot see and/or hear them. If older children are allowed to play outside unsupervised in your state, what policies are in place that provide for their well-being? Is the provider adhering to those policies? Do not allow your visit to be used as an excuse for a provider to avoid supervising the children in her program. Be sensitive to this issue. Strategize how you can reinforce good supervisory practices while conducting your visit.

UNCLEAN ENVIRONMENT

Home visitors should be able to recognize appropriate clutter and distinguish it from a dirty environment. If you see a home care setting that is obviously unclean, you need to bring it to the provider's attention, and she needs to address this issue.

UNSAFE ENVIRONMENT

Broken gates on stairways, peeling paint, broken railings or stairs, electrical outlets with no safety inserts, smoke and carbon monoxide alarms that do not work, broken or missing safety latches on drawers or doors where toxic materials are stored—this list could go on and on. One of the most difficult experiences is to be the professional who last visited a home in which a child was seriously hurt because of an accident that could have been prevented. It is the provider's job to maintain a healthy and safe environment at all times. It is your job to bring her attention to health and safety issues that pose potential danger.

LOTS OF TENSION

Many visual observations are straightforward: a clean or an unclean environment, sufficient or insufficient materials and equipment, engaged children or bored children. Tension and stress, on the other hand, are less straightforward. It amazes us that in most states, the child care application doesn't ask if the applicant actually likes children. Sometimes too much is assumed.

Tension in a child care environment is something you can usually see and feel. In identifying a tense child care setting, you can spot its symptoms: rigid body language, withdrawn children, lack of enthusiasm or joy. What you see, combined with your experience and good intuition, should tell you when something is seriously wrong.

 CHECKPOINT—Your Sense of Sight

During a home visit, ask yourself the following questions:

- What are your initial impressions? What do you see when you first enter the home? Are the children appropriately engaged with the provider, for example?

- Is the house clean and free of inappropriate clutter? Are its exterior and interior maintained properly?

- Are there sufficient materials and equipment for the children, and are they in good condition?

- What is the appearance of the provider and the children? Are they appropriately dressed for the season, for example?

- How effectively does the provider use her space?

- Does everyone present appear at ease: the provider, the children, and any household members present during the visit?

What You Feel

Every experienced home visitor has heard that little voice buried in her subconscious that sets off an alarm indicating that something is wrong. Sometimes it's not so much that something seems wrong as that something seems not quite right. An effective home visitor quickly learns the value of that inner voice and does not ignore it. Rather, she attempts to understand its origin.

Certain sensations are instinctive. The signal that tells us to flee from a dangerous situation is one of those. Being inquisitive is another. Home visitors often become inquisitive when things don't appear to be quite the way they should. This may occur when something you are seeing, hearing, or smelling does not match what the provider has described or shown you. To maintain the integrity of your visits, your safety, and the safety of participating children, you cannot ignore your feelings of discomfort. It may be that you do not feel comfortable confronting a provider you feel is not telling you the truth or attempting to mislead you. It may be a feeling of discomfort you pick up from the children in care. Whatever the reason, a necessary part of your job is to trust your instincts and to act on them when necessary.

In attempting to understand your feelings, it is important to identify the origin of your discomfort. To do this, take the time to analyze what is occurring. Do a quick inventory of your senses. Do you smell an odor, for example, that does not belong in a healthy and safe child care environment?

What do you hear? As you listen to the children talk with each other, do you hear something unpleasant or disturbing? As you listen to the provider, do you have doubts about the reliability of what she is sharing with you? Do you hear a tone of voice, an unkind word, a discussion between the provider and a household member or approved assistant that makes you uncomfortable?

What do you see? What is your first impression when you enter the child care environment? Is it not so much what you see but what you didn't see? Can you observe the entire environment, or does the provider prohibit you from doing so? Has she made available all of the appropriate paperwork for you to review, for example?

When attempting to identify what's activating your little voice, review every component of your visit. Do not be afraid to ask questions—or, in some cases, to re-ask questions. Occasionally when you ask a question, it is answered, but after you move on, you realize the answer does not make sense or does not match your observations. Don't be shy about asking your question again. It is perfectly appropriate to ask questions until you are convinced you understand the information conveyed.

Sometimes your feelings of discomfort may not be substantiated during your visit. In those instances, carefully document what occurred during your visit. If you feel the same level of discomfort after making a subsequent visit, talk with your supervisor. When an experienced home visitor's feelings of discomfort persist from visit to visit, something is usually wrong, and it should be identified.

 CHECKPOINT—Your Little Voice

When you feel uneasy, ask yourself the following questions:

- Did you attempt to identify the origin of your discomfort while you were still in the child care environment?

- Are you using tools that allow you to review all of the information the provider shared with you during your visit?

- Do you regularly confront providers in a professional manner when the information you have received does not coincide with what you see, smell, or hear?

- Are you sufficiently confident to speak with your supervisor when you feel that something is not right?

Manage Your
Time Well

Module Description

One of the greatest skills a home visitor can possess is the ability to manage time effectively. Making visits is a mandatory part of your profession. This module discusses all the best practices for maximizing the time allotted for visits and other job-related tasks. It presents practical technical assistance that will allow you to fully capitalize on your available time while still accomplishing your visit objectives.

As difficult as your job can be, many people depend on you to be prompt and efficient. When you employ skills that allow you to meet their expectations, you enhance all aspects of your professional life. (And one of the nicest results is that once you know how to use your time management skills successfully on the job, you can use them in your personal life as well.)

Learning Objectives

- Develop time management skills that allow you to complete all your work on time.
- Avoid feeling overwhelmed.
- Take control of your schedule.
- Maintain your motivation and positive attitude.
- Free up additional time.
- Effectively use deadlines.

. . . .

Case Study

Maria has scheduled a full day of visits tomorrow. As her day winds down, she takes some time to review her schedule beginning with her first appointment. Maria has scheduled a visit she anticipates will be time-consuming and perhaps challenging. She has learned from experience that it is always a good idea to schedule the most labor-intensive visits early in the day. She knows herself well, and she understands that to manage the rest of her day efficiently, she should get the most difficult tasks out of the way as early as possible. Maria smiles as she reviews the amount of time she has allotted for tomorrow morning's visit. Because she anticipates that this visit will take a bit longer than most, she has scheduled accordingly. She is glad she won't create any more anxiety for herself by running late and disrupting her entire day.

The next morning, when Maria arrives at her first visit, the provider immediately greets her and wants to discuss anything and everything that is not relevant to the visit. Maria has anticipated this tactic and in a calm and purposeful way refocuses the provider and stays on schedule.

When Maria completes this visit and returns to her car, she receives a call informing her that a visit scheduled for later that day has been canceled. Maria adjusts her schedule and makes the necessary changes to her calendar, which she carries with her whenever she is working.

Because Maria has scheduled realistically and is able to react to change immediately, at the end of the day she has successfully completed all of her scheduled assignments. She is pleased with the day and decides to reward herself by inviting a friend to dinner.

. . . .

Know Yourself

You know yourself better than anyone else does. Examine all the little things that may make effective time management difficult for you. For example, some people consistently put off doing what needs to be done until the last possible moment. Other people become so caught up in planning that when the time comes to implement their plan, they are so overwhelmed that they don't know where to begin. The following examples suggest how you may sabotage your time management. Consider the following information carefully; you may find that you use more than one strategy to mismanage your time. Identify your personality traits and find ways to make positive changes.

Procrastination

Of all the ways you can make the management of time difficult, procrastination tops the list. It is so very tempting to put that difficult visit off until the end of the day, the week, or better still, the month. But doing so will certainly not make the visit any easier. Wouldn't you love to delay doing paperwork, which is rarely anyone's favorite activity? Yet when paperwork is left to the last minute, it often becomes more difficult than it would have been if you completed it soon after a visit.

Everyone has had a day when getting into the car and driving to the first visit seems impossible because of the traffic, the weather, a head cold, or a simple lack of motivation. If you give in to that sense of futility, inevitably you will be faced with a month that has somehow flown by with many visits not made and too little time remaining to do them properly. You may find yourself putting as much energy into rescheduling visits or finding reasons to postpone them than it would have taken to complete the visits in the first place.

If you are a procrastinator, you should take the necessary steps to eliminate this pattern of behavior. Eliminating procrastination does not occur magically or immediately; it takes work. It also requires some very specific planning on your part.

When you catch yourself procrastinating, ask yourself what you are trying to avoid. *Approach avoidance* is something most people experience at one time or another: it is not uncommon to want to postpone experiences that you do not look forward to. Some visits are simply less pleasant than others. Some paperwork is predictably tedious. But you should probe more deeply: Are you fearful of possible confrontation during a difficult visit? Is there something about the paperwork that you do not understand, so you are unsure about how to proceed? You must identify the underlying reason for putting off a task in order to correct it. If you are procrastinating because it has simply become a habit, you can help rid yourself of this bad habit through the following approaches.

START WITH THE MOST DIFFICULT TASKS FIRST

If you are in the habit of putting off your most difficult tasks to the last possible moment—a visit with a difficult provider, for example—recognize that all this accomplishes is to extend your periods of stress. If you tackle challenging visits or tasks first, you can plan more effectively. You may even find you actually experience less dread in the course of your day, week, or month. Another benefit of addressing the most difficult tasks first is that you often discover that they aren't quite as bad as you anticipated. Even in those rare cases when a task is as bad as you thought it would be, once it's completed, you can move on to more pleasant activities.

FIND TIME TO FOCUS ON HIGH-PRIORITY ACTIVITIES

If your job involves more than conducting home visits, and it usually does, you should decide which work activities should be given priority status. Not every task you are responsible for has the same importance or timeline. You must accomplish your difficult tasks as soon as possible, but you also need to complete other assignments prioritized by your organization. When considering how to schedule your visits, identify which ones are high priority. Consult your supervisor regarding this if necessary. Complaint investigations, for example, usually take priority over other types of monitoring visits. Since it is your job to assure that high-priority visits are conducted in a timely fashion, you need to identify and schedule them as quickly as possible.

CONCENTRATE ON ONE THING AT A TIME

At times you may find yourself procrastinating not because you choose to but because you are so busy thinking about everything you need to do that you can't figure out how to get started. Once you have prioritized your tasks and created your schedule, focus on your first task, finish it, and then focus on the next, and finish that. Some people find it helpful to cross off each completed activity on a written list. Often the most difficult part is taking that first step. If you reward yourself in some way, you can often find sufficient motivation to get started.

Disorganization

In balancing all the tasks that are included in your job description, you may sometimes feel overwhelmed. Some fundamental steps you can take will help you take control of your schedule:

- Begin by obtaining a calendar if you do not currently have one. If you have a calendar and don't currently use it, start.
- Look at the month ahead and schedule the visits you know you need to make. Be certain you are creating a flexible schedule that evenly distributes your visits throughout the month. A monthly

calendar allows you to see clearly if there are too many visits for the last week of the month. Adjust as necessary to assure you are not setting yourself up for failure.

- Once you have organized your schedule for the month with the visits you need to make, look at the visits you would like to make. Examine your weekly schedule. Ask yourself if you have allocated sufficient time for each visit. Have you looked at your travel time? Have you allotted sufficient time for transitions? Are you balancing your time in the field with enough time in the office to complete your paperwork? Is there a way to integrate any additional visits, or should you be reducing the number of proposed visits based on your calculations?

- Review your plans each morning or the night before and set priorities for yourself. The best-laid plans do not always work the way they should. A home visitor cannot control the weather, for example. Develop and maintain a list of specific things to be done each day, prioritize them, and schedule the most important ones as early in the day as you can. A realistic daily schedule helps you exercise control over your time and allows you to make changes when necessary.

The habits that promote your procrastination or disorganization are usually ones you can correct. Your workload or work environment may affect your day-to-day ability to correct counterproductive habits. If this is the case, ask for assistance. Don't be shy about asking if some tasks can be delegated to other people.

Keep a Positive Outlook

To believe you can manage your time effectively, you must feel positive and motivated. One of the best ways to motivate yourself is to find something you enjoy in everything you do. You are less likely to procrastinate when you are actually looking forward to making a home visit. Finding something you enjoy in each home visit also helps you maintain a positive attitude during even the most difficult visits. For example, you may enjoy interacting with young children. You may, in fact, enjoy the children a great deal more than you enjoy the provider. If that focus allows you to schedule a visit with positive anticipation, use it to your advantage. When creating your schedule, try to find at least one positive thing in each task—even if it is simply knowing that once the task is completed you have another month before you have to think about it again! Sometimes it is helpful to remember that your job is generally not a boring one. There is something to be said about the ability to be outside of an office, enjoying the weather, and anticipating a unique experience in each home you visit.

Another way you can motivate yourself is to think about what you *can* do rather than what you can't. For example, if you have scheduled four visits, believe that you can accomplish what you have planned. If one of your four clients happens to be to a provider who has a history of noncompliances, consider what you can bring with you to assist her and to move the visit along in a positive and expeditious way. If you and a provider have a negative history, you may feel every future visit will be negative. This can become a self-fulfilling prophecy: you may be setting yourself up to find it more difficult to schedule a visit in that home and more difficult to manage your time effectively while you're there. Instead, keep an open mind and an optimistic attitude and believe that every visit has the potential to be successful. It is a much better plan to expect the positive rather than to always anticipate the negative.

Finding ways to build on your success also helps you maintain a positive outlook. Successes are not always large or dramatic, but each success is significant. For example, if your morning goes well and runs according to schedule, acknowledge that success and attempt to carry it over into your afternoon.

To maintain a positive outlook, stop regretting your failures and start learning from your mistakes. If you have a tendency to overschedule your day, for example, and you never seem able to accomplish all you need to do, stop and consider. Why can't you achieve your goals? Is it because your expectations do not match the reality of your job? If so and your visits are as long as they need to be, develop a schedule that more realistically reflects your job expectations. If the problem is rather that you are conducting your visits in ways that don't allow you to complete each assignment as you had originally planned, look at each visit and determine if you are using your time effectively. Strategize about what you can do during the visit to use your time more efficiently.

Have confidence in yourself and your judgment. You are the person who best understands exactly what your job involves. Have confidence that you can do your job successfully. Don't get discouraged if you find you haven't accomplished everything you expected to. Give your schedule a chance to work. Make adjustments only after you have given yourself sufficient opportunity to succeed.

A great motivator for maintaining a positive attitude is rewarding yourself when your plan succeeds. This is especially useful when completing important tasks in a timely manner. Allow yourself to feel good about your daily, weekly, and monthly accomplishments. Find creative ways to reward yourself when you have done exactly what you set out to do. Think of Maria in our case study. Maria had a good day because she planned ahead, was prepared to make changes if necessary, and accomplished everything she wanted and needed to. Because she used her time wisely, Maria allowed herself a reward. In doing so, she gave herself even more motivation to manage her time well every day.

Begin with Good Planning

Good planning cannot be overemphasized. To manage your time, you need to control it. One of the ways to do this is by planning each workday in each workweek in each work month. This may sound tedious, but once you acquire this habit, you will wonder how you ever functioned without it. Planning allows you to look realistically at what you need to do and then attach a corresponding block of time to each task and activity.

Time management does not begin when you visit; it starts long before you arrive. It should have started when you created your schedule for the upcoming month, week, and day. It continues before you ever reach the home and is reflected in your identification of what you plan to bring and what you need to communicate.

Look ahead. Use all of the resources available to you while you create your work plan. Be aware of extended weather forecasts, for example, because you do not want to drive long distances in a storm. Be aware of any other mandatory commitments that may influence your schedule, such as meetings or trainings that you need to attend. Looking ahead and keeping informed helps you to plan and to create more options for yourself.

Use All of Your Time Efficiently

It's not only important to focus on one thing at a time but also to do one thing at a time. In this day of multitasking, adults have a tendency to try to accomplish as many activities as possible simultaneously. Sometimes this approach works; often, however, it does not. Accomplishing one task before moving on to the next one results in a wise and productive use of your time. This is especially true during a home visit. When conducting a visit, you should focus on the task at hand and not the three visits to follow.

Other opportunities for efficient use of time present themselves when you are consistently looking for ways to free up available time. As a simple example, when you are visiting a new client, obtain accurate driving directions prior to leaving your office or home. Good preparation before any visit allows you to free up additional time. Look at how you collect data while in a home, for example. Are there data collection tools, such as checklists, that might allow you to use time more effectively?

Catch yourself when you are not being productive. While visiting a provider, for example, you may find yourself repeating the same information over and over. Stop! Pull back and give some thought to how you can conduct your visit more effectively. Does the provider not understand what you're trying to communicate, or is she simply not listening? In addressing the possible reasons for repeating information, you will ultimately be able to save yourself time. Look at your visits closely. Where is the greatest amount of time spent? Are there ways to conduct your visits in a more streamlined and efficient fashion? Do not be afraid to experiment. You may decide that reviewing required paperwork first before observing the environment will allow you to progress more quickly. Try it!

Distraction might also be an issue in your workplace. Are there coworkers or activities that create a distraction in your work setting, making it difficult for you to complete your tasks? When you feel yourself being unproductive, think about why and what you need to do to change the situation. Are there areas of your workplace or times of day that are better suited for you to do your paperwork? If so, implement a change in your schedule. Perhaps you are better able to accomplish your paperwork requirements at home, in your car, or at a public library. Discuss options with your supervisor.

Give Yourself Feedback

Keep track of your successes, even when they appear to be minor. Your own feedback can be invaluable. As you establish goals for yourself, make sure you identify milestones along the way that will help you work toward achieving your goals. Acknowledge each time you meet a milestone. When you have a planned workday that has gone according to schedule, pat yourself on the back. In the same vein, it is also important to acknowledge when you cannot meet your schedule. This helps you to stop and ask yourself why and to make any adjustments.

Push yourself and be persistent, especially when you know you are doing well. When you are acting on your monthly schedule and are on target, persist. Congratulate yourself on creating and maintaining a schedule that works well for you.

Be sure to set deadlines for yourself whenever possible. In most professions, deadlines are imposed by employers. Establishing your own deadlines can be beneficial, because doing so gives you additional control over prioritizing your work. Deadlines also create a mechanism for feedback: either you have met your deadline or you have not; that is very straightforward feedback that allows you to plan more effectively next time.

Put It in Writing

Think on paper whenever possible. Doing your thinking on paper makes review and revision easier. It is far easier to erase a written thought that isn't exactly what you feel it should be than to retract something said without sufficient forethought. Once you get in the habit of thinking on paper, you will find this an effective strategy for outlining your objectives. Keep a written schedule and make written adjustments to your calendar. Writing provides a reliable and tangible reminder while allowing you to successfully organize your thoughts.

When you begin introducing time management strategies, remember to keep track of how long each of your daily activities takes as well as the time used for preplanning. It then becomes easier to project the time you should realistically allot in the future.

Many people have eliminated handwritten schedules. Many home visitors organize their schedules with a wide range of devices. What matters is not so much how you keep a record of your time but that you do keep one. Whether you use a personal digital assistant (PDA) or a pen, you'll find that good time management involves the same elements: thoughtful consideration, planning, flexibility, perseverance, feedback, and the willingness to ask for assistance.

CHECKPOINT—Time Management

Answer the following questions to determine where you could use more efficient time management:

- Do you plan in order to keep tasks and your visit schedule from getting out of control?

- Do you put daily plans on paper (or your electronic device) and carry them with you?

- Is your plan flexible?

- How often do you accomplish all you plan to do in a day?

- Do you allocate time in a way that allows you to accomplish all of your most important objectives?

Module 4

Maintain a Balance of Authority

Module Description

Home visitors usually enter a client's home to determine the client's compliance with rules and regulations. From the moment you pass through the door, the balance of power is established: as a home visitor, you are in a position of authority. One of the most difficult problems for many home visitors is the question of how not to misuse their authority. Your ability to be sensitive to the provider and the participating children can be a double-edged sword. Your empathy allows you to perform your tasks in an appropriate manner; at the same time, knowing that your visit may bring discomfort can be troubling. In some instances, you may try to protect yourself by creating a stern and authoritarian persona. This does not usually produce effective or desired results. At the other end of the spectrum are visitors who may become so caught up in attempting to make everyone happy that the focus of their visit is lost and they become ineffective.

This module is meant to assist you in identifying your personal style while providing you with information to help you achieve an appropriate balance when entering a child care setting. Aggressive bullying, sniping, mindless obstructionism, capricious decision making, general disrespect, and an unwillingness to listen to any voice but your own are examples of how authority can be misused. When authority is misused, it may stop others from achieving their goals. An improper balance of authority can create poor morale, and it may cause clients to terminate their affiliation with your organization. Included in this module is information that relates specifically to male home visitors, as well.

Balance of authority is a topic that has special relevance for men in this field, especially when considering that the large majority of family child care providers are women.

Learning Objectives

- Be comfortable with the level of authority you take on as a home visitor.
- Avoid behavior that is overpowering, intimidating, or coercive.
- Be empathetic while maintaining professionalism.
- Take responsibility.
- Assess your role if a visit does not go as well as you had planned.
- Understand the value of client feedback.

· · · · · · · · · ·

Case Study

· ·

Marco is a home visitor and one of the few males employed by his organization. He is responsible for monitoring approximately thirty homes. In each home there is a female family child care provider. Marco has often felt more than the normal level of scrutiny and defensive behavior during his home visits.

Someone else in Marco's office has scheduled a monitoring visit for him with a new provider. Since he has not been to this home before and has not talked by phone with the provider, he is unsure if she realizes that her home visitor is a man.

Marco has given some careful thought to how he will dress for this visit. He wants to appear professional, and he also wants to dress in a way that is comfortable but will not appear intimidating. Marco chooses not to wear a suit; instead, he wears a crisp, collared shirt and slacks.

Marco has thought about what he wants to accomplish during this initial visit. He wants to let the provider know that he is a resource and someone she can call with questions. He wants the provider to understand that he will not attempt to intimidate or misuse his authority. At the same time, he needs to communicate his responsibilities while in the home. He will reinforce that his responsibilities include effectively communicating his organization's contractual requirements as well as the licensing requirements governing how the provider operates her business.

When Marco arrives at the home, he waits patiently on the front steps for the provider to answer the door. When she does, she makes it clear that not only was she unaware his organization was sending a male home visitor, but she is also somewhat uncomfortable with this idea. Before entering her home, Marco explains his professional role as a representative of his organization. In doing so, he moves the emphasis away from himself and appropriately places it on his professional obligation while in her home. He acknowledges her apparent discomfort with the visit and respectfully informs her of her options.

As Marco enters the home at the provider's invitation, he respectfully follows his client. He allows her to direct him to the place she wants to meet. He gives her time to think about where she will be most comfortable, and he is patient as she attempts to identify the appropriate setting for this visit.

During this interview, Marco is cautious about his tone and body language. He sits at the kitchen counter with his client rather than standing. Marco appears comfortable without being too casual. He has brought necessary and helpful information. He reinforces his role as someone who wants to be a resource for the client. He does not patronize or condescend to her. He asks appropriate questions and demonstrates his sincere interest in the provider's child care program.

Before leaving, Marco reiterates his role. He tells the client what to expect during the next visit. He helps her understand that his role as a monitor requires him to observe her child care program and her child care setting. He is polite and courteous as he leaves the provider's home. He remembers to ask if the client has any questions or concerns.

· · · · · · · · ·

The Image You Present

The image you project is perhaps the most powerful message a provider receives when you enter her home. It is to your advantage to demonstrate professionalism and respect. Often when the initial impression you make is less than positive, your message, no matter how well communicated, is lost. Be mindful of your image and consider the following.

Dress

Your appearance sets a tone. Do not overdress. Dress comfortably and professionally—not in a manner that is overpowering or distinctly out of place. Your clothes should complement the environment you are assessing. Wearing an expensive fur coat on a home visit, for example, would not on most occasions be an appropriate choice of outerwear. You also need to be cautious about overcompensating and dressing down. You may visit a provider who, because she is working in her home with small children, does not pay close attention to her attire. Your job is not her job—you need to pay attention to what you wear. Your example of appropriate rather than intimidating or patronizing dress plays an important part in your role as a home visitor. See Module 1 for more information about appropriate attire.

Verbal Communication

How do you speak? When providing technical assistance, do you offer suggestions or do you give orders? Your tone says a great deal about how you choose to manage your authority. Speak respectfully.

Do you actually listen to the client when she responds to a question? Listening not only signifies respect; it is also an important part of good communication. Although the primary purpose of your visit is to assess a provider's business, you should always remember that you are in her home. Never attempt to humiliate, denigrate, or embarrass a client during your visit. If you observe something that is inappropriate, communicate your observations to her in a moderate and professional manner. Accusations or personal attacks are not within the framework of appropriate communication between you and a provider.

Body Language

What about your body language? Balance of authority is based on openness and mutual understanding. If you enter a client's home with a frown on your face and a rigid, aggressive stance, you do not enhance feelings of comfort or collaboration. Think about the relaxed and respectful way in which Marco presented himself in the case study. His conscious efforts to put the provider at ease while maintaining his professionalism smoothed an awkward situation.

When you are uncomfortable or anticipate a negative visit, your body language frequently sends a significant message before you can speak a word. If you are feeling defensive, identify what is causing those feelings before making the visit. Where you believe your personal safety is concerned, it is important to identify why you feel uneasy and what can be done to alleviate your apprehension. When you identify feelings of discomfort, think about when and why they occur and how you can effectively deal with them. Home visitors who misuse their authority often do so as a protective mechanism.

Define Boundaries

How do you define your goals as a home visitor? To establish a good balance of authority, you must be clear about your objectives. If you know a collaborative effort will result in better child care, you are better able to participate in positive teamwork. If, instead, you see your role predominately as the person whose job it is to point out deficiencies and failures, you place yourself in a different position. The optimal goal of assessment is a positive outcome. If you do not find ways to work collaboratively on a positive outcome and you narrow your evaluation only to areas of noncompliance, you contribute to an imbalance of authority. That imbalance makes your job more difficult.

On occasion, you may confuse establishing appropriate professional boundaries with balancing your position of authority. Although it is important to establish professional boundaries—for example, appropriate topics of discussion and avoiding compromising behavior—you should also be mindful of your position of authority. Your role as a home visitor gives you automatic authority from the moment you walk into a home. Consequently, acknowledging your client's empowerment is helpful in establishing a reasonable balance in your working relationship. Be polite, have a positive attitude, and compliment the client on the environment or program when you can—these actions do not compromise professional boundaries. They allow the client to see you as an objective observer. Don't lose track of your personality while establishing appropriate professional boundaries. A client should not be so intimidated by your presence that she is unable to share polite conversation with you. Nor should you be so caught up in your position that you are unable to respond in a civil manner. Conversations should not compromise confidentiality or consist primarily of gossip; neither should they serve as distractions from the focus of your visit. Polite conversation means exactly what it implies: it allows the provider to understand that although you are in her home for professional reasons, you are civil and respectful of her role and her environment.

Try not to be patronizing or condescending. Although you may provide instruction and technical assistance, do not assume you are more intelligent or superior to a provider because of this. It is your job to have specific types of information and to be able to share it in an understandable fashion. It is the provider's job to offer quality child care. Keep in mind that while your strengths may not be a provider's strengths, the opposite is probably true as well. If you find that a client is defensive and guarded during your visit, think about what and how you are communicating. Very few people respond well when they feel they are being spoken down to.

Specific Strategies

Here are some helpful hints for balancing your authority. Keep strategies like these constantly in mind to help achieve and maintain balance; doing so makes your job easier.

When in Doubt, Ask

If you sense that the client is uncomfortable, ask why. Be cautious; you do not want your inquiry to sound like an inquisition. Ask politely if she has concerns about working with you or with something about your visit. This is a good way to open discussion that can help clarify confusions or misconceptions. Do not, however, compromise your ability to do your job objectively. Providers need to understand that you are in their home to monitor their business and that responsibility cannot be avoided.

Leave Any Preconceived Notions at the Door

On occasion you may find yourself making assumptions before ever entering a child care program. This is faulty procedure, and it can undermine your visit. You do not want to enter a provider's home with defensive or overly assertive body language. Nor do you want to enter a provider's home unprepared to deal with issues you may encounter. A client's response frequently mirrors the message she receives from you. Stop yourself before drawing any unsubstantiated conclusions until you have conducted your visit. Part of your professional role is to demonstrate that you enter each program with an open mind.

Keep Your Hands to Yourself

This sounds too obvious even to mention. Yet many people frequently touch others in the course of a conversation to reassure or to reinforce a point. Don't.

Touching signals a personal connection that does not necessarily exist between you and the client. This is especially true when the home visitor is male and the client is a woman. An innocent action can easily be misconstrued. The no-touching rule extends to the children in the program. Parents enrolling children in child care do not expect their children to disclose at the end of the day that they were held or touched by a stranger, even if the stranger was a home visitor. You can be friendly and supportive without touching.

Be Patient

The life of a child care provider can be hectic. Children in care frequently act their worst when the home visitor arrives. A provider's first responsibility always must be the well-being of the children in her home. Allow her time to redirect and appropriately support the children so you can successfully conduct your business. Identifying tasks such as reviewing required paperwork can give the provider an opportunity to organize the children while you conduct your visit. Behaviors like constantly looking at your watch or the clock, crossing your arms and tapping your foot, or sighing to indicate your impatience are not only unfair but extremely counterproductive. If the provider's home is chaotic during each visit, you can certainly tailor your technical assistance to help her overcome disorganization.

Engage in Periodic Self-Assessment

One of the pitfalls you should try to avoid in establishing balance is what we refer to as the "my way or the highway" approach. Although regulations and contractual language bolster your position, remember that no one is perfect, including you.

To maintain an appropriate balance of authority, use the people skills we discuss throughout this manual. How do clients respond to you when you speak? How good are your antennae at picking up important signals? Are you sensitive when a client becomes stressed by your visit? Do you acknowledge that supervising children effectively while responding to your questions may produce some anxiety? Are you able to get to the point and offer realistic options when discussing problems? Most people do not wholly enjoy being evaluated, and not every provider is going to be overjoyed to see you at the door. But if the majority of your visits are unpleasant and you find yourself constantly confronting providers in an adversarial manner, something is very wrong. Periodically, use the information in this manual to evaluate your home visiting approach. This will help ensure that your message is not lost in your delivery.

Be Aware

For your own personal safety, be alert and aware when you are in a family child care home. You should always be aware of a provider's body language as well as the behavior of the children during a home visit. What do you see? Does the provider appear to be nervous when you enter the home? Are the children apprehensive when you visit? When people feel inadequate or disempowered, which is what an imbalance of authority can create, their tone of voice and body language can become rigid and defensive. Some providers will go so far as to become aggressive in the hope that if they take the offensive, you will back off. Be aware of these signals so you can make adjustments quickly.

Do Your Homework

Being informed always provides you with an advantage. Part of your preparation for a visit should be an assessment of a client's history with your organization. Issues of authority usually arise when home visitors are caught off-guard. When you are well informed and well prepared, overemphasizing your authority is seldom necessary.

Overcompensation

Sometimes you may not feel comfortable with your position and the authority it often entails. You may be extremely sensitive to the fact that when you visit a client you are the cause of some discomfort. In some instances, this will occur no matter how you frame your visit. It is common to want the people you work with to like you. But during home visits, you must remember your role. You have a job to do. It is not in your or the client's best interest to conduct your visits in ways that polarize. Neither should you avoid tasks that are part of your job because you do not want to offend or make a client dislike you. You are certainly not helping yourself professionally, and you are not helping the client either. If you conduct your visits appropriately and the client takes exception to you because you have identified her noncompliance, so be it. You do a great deal of harm to your own authority and the authority of other professionals when you decide to overcompensate and look the other way. Do not put yourself in that position.

A Special Note for Male Home Visitors

While the skills presented in this manual are equally useful to men and women, men in the home visiting profession face unique issues and challenges. In some ways, the balance of authority issue is most challenging for male home visitors.

Most providers caring for children in their homes are female. If you are a man, you have probably found that on occasion there are some female clients who may not appear to feel as comfortable talking with you as they would with a female home visitor. Men frequently communicate differently than women. Even your nonverbal language may be perceived differently. For example, while a female home visitor may appear to look stern, you may be perceived as threatening or intimidating when you exhibit the very same type of expression or body language.

Extended family can also create a more complex dynamic for you. Some husbands feel uncomfortable with having an unfamiliar man in their home. Some ethnic groups consider it improper for a man to visit a female, especially if she is married and her husband is not present.

For these reasons, you should pay particular attention to balance of authority. Work on developing a sensitivity that will help you to anticipate problems before they become too big to handle. Discuss when you sense misunderstanding or false assumptions. Carefully document what occurs during your home visits. Do not place yourself in positions of vulnerability. Trust your instincts, and do not be afraid to terminate your visit and leave a home if you feel a provider is overly defensive or is responding to your presence in an inappropriate manner.

CHECKPOINT—Balance of Authority

Examine the following questions before and during your visits:

- Do you carefully think about what you will wear on days you make home visits?

- Do you prepare what you will say and how you will say it?

- Do you review the goals set for the provider and think about how you can support her?

- Do you think about the provider's strengths and how you can support her in using those strengths to meet goals?

- How do you feel during each visit? Are you uneasy? Examine your feelings. If something is bothering you, define what it is and try to alleviate those feelings.

Be an Effective Communicator

Module Description

Understanding the communication process and the different ways people communicate is vital for a home visitor. Many of the problems that occur during a home visit are the result of you and the provider failing to communicate effectively. In this module, we discuss the following aspects of communication:

- Communication styles—how you speak to providers and how a provider's communication style can affect you.
- Listening skills—why listening is a vital part of communication and how this can affect your message.
- Nonverbal and body language—how your body supports or contradicts your words and how to interpret a provider's body language.

As a home visitor, your communication with the provider directly reflects on how your organization is perceived by the public. Effective communication will

- increase the provider's comfort level,
- guarantee that your message is received,
- assist you in accomplishing your goals and the goals of your organization, and
- ensure retention of providers.

This module identifies and explains the skills and techniques that are important for you to use to effectively communicate your message in the field.

Learning Objectives

- Understand the benefits and potential negatives of your communication style.
- Recognize the communication styles of your clients.
- Become comfortable relating to communication styles that are different from your own.
- Be able to acknowledge a client's point of view without agreeing with it.
- Effectively use "I" messages.
- Know the difference between listening and hearing.
- Be aware of your own body language when you are visiting a client.
- Recognize defensive body language.

• • • • • • • • •

Case Study

Nadine has been encouraging her client Jana to introduce new foods to the children in her care. All six children are three- to five-year-olds and participants in the Child and Adult Care Food Program (CACFP). Jana receives a food reimbursement check for feeding meals based on certain food components to the children in her care.

Nadine has noticed from Jana's records over the past months that she feeds the children the same combination of foods every week. She often serves chicken fingers and fries for several days in a row. Nadine has also noted that Jana feeds the children only two different fruits and two different vegetables, alternating them every other day. Since first noticing these trends, Nadine has addressed the issue of food variety in each of her visits.

Nadine is puzzled that Jana still has not introduced new foods to the children. Just last month, Nadine brought a wonderfully illustrated pamphlet describing the importance of introducing new foods to the children. Nadine quickly went over the main points and then gave Jana the task of finding new foods to feed the children. Jana looked over the information when Nadine handed it to her. She said she understood the importance of varying her menu. Nadine felt good about the visit and was sure she would see a change in Jana's meal patterns. After all, Nadine reasoned, she had clearly told Jana what she needed to do. Nadine felt she had even kept the subject on track when Jana had tried to explain why she fed the children what she did. Nadine did not want to hear excuses and had clearly asked Jana if she was going to meet the task and offer the children more variety. Jana agreed that she would.

Today Nadine is in the office, checking her client's menus. She is particularly interested in seeing how well Jana has performed the task she has given her. She is shocked to see that Jana has not introduced one new food during the whole month. At first, Nadine feels very discouraged and plans on confronting Jana the next day. As Nadine thinks about it further, she wonders what has gone wrong. She believes she clearly communicated the need for Jana to make changes. She is also sure that Jana had agreed to comply. Nadine is puzzled; she knows that somehow she is not communicating with Jana productively. She decides to ask her supervisor for another perspective.

Nadine meets with her supervisor, Carla, later in the day. She explains the situation and asks for Carla's opinion. Carla thinks about what she knows about Nadine. She knows that Nadine is a quick thinker and acts decisively when presented with a task. She also knows that Nadine can be impatient and often does not listen to other people when she has her mind made up about something.

Next Carla thinks about Jana. Carla knows Jana well, for they live in the same community. In fact, Carla has worked with Jana on a few school committee projects. She knows that Jana is well liked. People find her easy to talk to. She also knows that Jana tends to back down when confronted with unpleasant situations and that she has a hard time saying no.

Carla recognizes that Nadine and Jana's communication styles may not work well together. She suggests to Nadine that she change her approach when speaking to Jana. She reminds Nadine that the home visitor's job is to adapt her style to accommodate the provider—not the other way around.

Carla asks Nadine to consider what she knows about Jana. While they discuss Jana, Carla points out things that help Nadine identify Jana's communication style. Then Carla restates Nadine's goal: Jana should feed a greater variety of foods to the children. Carla asks Nadine if she asked Jana specific questions about this goal. Nadine admits she basically gave Jana the task without giving her a chance to speak. Carla points out that Jana does not like confrontations: she may have agreed simply because she didn't want to create an unpleasant situation.

With Carla's help, Nadine plans how to be more sensitive to Jana's style of communicating during the next home visit. She knows she should not ask yes/no questions. Instead, she needs to ask probing questions and then really listen to Jana's answers.

The next day Nadine visits Jana. When Jana lets her in, Nadine asks if she can sit with her for a few minutes and discuss Jana's menus. Jana agrees. Nadine tells Jana she has noticed that Jana is still having a hard time feeding the children more variety in their meals. Jana nods her head yes. Nadine next asks Jana if she understands the importance of feeding the children new foods, and again Jana nods her head yes. Nadine asks Jana if she would like her to help Jana make a menu that would introduce a new fruit next week. Once again, Jana nods her head. Nadine works with Jana for the next few minutes, making a menu that introduces a new fruit and vegetable during the month. When they are finished, Nadine asks Jana if she will use the menu and try the new foods. Again, Jana nods in agreement.

Even though Nadine thinks this is going well, she remembers that Jana often has agreed to making changes and then has not carried them out. She also notes that Jana has not had very much to say during this meeting. She decides to ask a couple of probing questions to see if she can determine how Jana really feels. She asks Jana what obstacles she sees in implementing the new menus. Jana is quiet for a moment. Then she tells Nadine that she has two children from the same family who are very picky eaters. Their parents only feed them a very limited variety of foods. When she attempts to introduce a different food, the children get upset and refuse to eat. They have reported this to their mother in the past, and she has insisted that Jana feed the children what they like. Jana admits she does not know what to do.

Nadine is very happy she has probed a little deeper. She now has a clear sense of Jana's problem. Nadine tells Jana she has information on picky eaters that she will bring for Jana to read. She will also put together a packet of information on the importance of introducing new foods to children so Jana can give it to the parents.

Nadine feels very satisfied with the outcome of her visit with Jana. Changing her communication style to fit Jana's has given her a deeper understanding of Jana. Nadine is now confident that she will be able to support Jana in a more meaningful way.

· · · · · · · ·

Effective Communication

When a sender transmits an idea to a receiver, that's communication. Effective communication occurs only if the receiver understands what the sender intended to transmit. The communication process has three steps:

1. Thought: information exists in the sender's mind. Examples include concepts, ideas, information, feelings.
2. Encoding: a message is sent to the recipient using words or other symbols of communication.
3. Decoding: the recipient translates the words or symbols into terms she can understand.

When you speak to clients during your home visits, they receive two types of information: content and context. Content is the actual words or symbols of the message, whether you give the information to the provider orally, in a written letter, or in a handout. Everyone uses and interprets the meanings of words differently. Therefore, even though you know what you are saying, it can be understood differently. Even the simplest messages can be misunderstood. Further confusing the message, many words have multiple meanings.

Context is the way the message is delivered—it includes the tone of voice, the look in the sender's eyes, body language, hand gestures, and emotions (anger, fear, uncertainty, confidence, etc.). Context often causes messages to be misunderstood, because people commonly believe what they see rather than what they hear. They are more likely to trust the accuracy of nonverbal than verbal behaviors.

Keeping these points in mind, you need to look at how people communicate and how to accommodate your own message to their different communication styles.

Communication Styles

Have you ever wondered why you seem to click with some clients while others frustrate you? Have you found that what works with one person does not necessarily work with another? The reason is simple. Everyone is unique. Everyone has his or her own personality and ways of interacting with people. Occasionally your style of communication may directly conflict with someone else's, making your message difficult to get across. Learning to see how your style of communication interacts with the styles of others gives you a greater understanding of clients' negative or positive responses. You want clients to know you understand them. Whether you agree with their points of view or not, you open the door to communication by validating their feelings.

As you read about the following communication styles, try to identify your own style of communication. Knowing how you communicate is just as important as understanding the styles of the providers you visit. Notice that certain combinations of styles conflict with one another.

Independent Irma

Independent Irma often makes quick decisions and talks fast. Irma may be a poor listener. She can easily see the big picture and becomes impatient with those who do not. Irma has provided services for many years and believes she already knows everything you have to tell her. She can be tactless and willingly states that she does not need you to tell her anything, because she is capable of doing things by herself.

How can you accommodate Irma's communication style? When talking to Irma, stick to the subject. Do not add a lot of unnecessary information. Remember that a person like Irma believes she can do a better job by herself, so she will not welcome your opinion on how something should be done. You need to acknowledge Irma's many years of experience and ask for her input to achieve any goal you recommend. By discussing options with her and deciding collaboratively on a course of action, you validate Irma's abilities and years of experience. Here's an example: On your home visits to Irma's house, you observe that the children are often sitting in front of the TV. Your goal is to encourage Irma to turn off the TV and supervise an age-appropriate activity. You explain your organization's goal of trying to raise the awareness of providers about scheduling age-appropriate activities. You give Irma information and handouts on the importance of age-appropriate opportunities for learning during the day. You also acknowledge Irma's experience and ask if she has suggestions to share with new providers. You then ask her how she will reach this new goal.

Chatty Cathy

This type of person loves people and loves to talk. Cathy is the client who will tell you her life history and the history of everyone in her family. Cathy likes to make jokes, and it is hard to get her to take your conversations seriously. She is expressive and fun, and she loves to be the center of attention.

How do you accommodate Cathy's communication style? You should spend a few minutes socializing; this is important to Cathy. But you must limit socializing and take control of the conversation. Cathy likes a lot of praise and acknowledgment. If you comment on something positive you notice about her child care, you may be able to turn the conversation toward your visit's purpose. Cathy does not like to work alone. When proposing new ideas or changes to her, use plural pronouns—"Let us" or "we" instead of "you." Here's an example: You notice the children are often in front of the TV at Cathy's house too. You approach Cathy by discussing the information on scheduling age-appropriate activities. You praise her for her activities with the children, and then you suggest working together to plan more activities for the children's schedule. Together you discuss a new schedule. Then you follow up with a phone call during the week to see how Cathy is implementing the schedule. You continue to praise her progress during each successive visit.

Agreeable Annie

Annie is laid back. She does not like confrontation and may agree with you just to avoid an argument. Annie is a good listener and sensitive to others. Her sensitivity can cause problems because she tries to balance pleasing every parent with complying with every regulation. Annie generally will not tell you how she really feels. Nor will she ask for help. She does not make decisions quickly; she needs time to think things over. Annie has a hard time saying no and may agree to a task or change she does not fully understand or finds difficult to accomplish. Do you recognize Annie? In the case study that opened this module, Jana communicates in this style.

How can you accommodate Annie's communication style? You need to be especially careful not to ask yes/no questions. Instead, ask questions that will elicit a detailed response. When instituting a policy or procedure, go over each part of the instructions and make sure Annie fully understands it. Help her create a plan to accomplish the task. Giving Annie a timeline or deadline is helpful. Remember to ask if Annie needs help, because she probably will not ask for it.

Here's an example: You are trying to explain to Annie that she needs to cut down on the children's TV watching and conduct more age-appropriate activities. After giving Annie the reasons, you do not ask, "Do you understand?" Annie will most likely respond, "Yes." Instead, ask her for specifics: "How do you plan to schedule the activities?" You may have to keep asking questions until you know she understands every part of the task. If there is any part she is not clear about, offer a suggestion and examples. When you are convinced that Annie understands, ask, "When do you think you can initiate this change?"

Factual Fred

People like Fred are very cautious. Fred likes to get all the facts and details before he acts or speaks. Often Fred can be a perfectionist. He does not freely show his emotions, so you may find it difficult to know what he is thinking.

How can you accommodate Fred's communication style? A provider like Fred needs to know the facts and reasons behind any changes or suggestions you are offering. Conduct research before you visit this provider, and bring handouts or copies of regulations that substantiate your recommendations. Doing so ensures that Fred will be receptive. Remember, he does not necessarily want your opinion on how something should be done, but he will respect facts that back up your request. Here's an example: You know you must prepare before visiting Fred. If you want Fred to conduct age-appropriate activities instead of TV watching, do not say, "I *think* the children watch too much TV" or "I *think* you should have more activities." Fred is not interested in your opinion. He may not think the children watch too much TV at all. Instead, refer to your prepared facts and handouts: "Looking at these facts and figures, how do you plan to adjust your schedule to include more activities?"

Your Communication Style

Just as important as recognizing how Independent Irma, Chatty Cathy, Agreeable Annie, and Factual Fred communicate is knowing your own style. Ask yourself the following questions.

HOW QUICKLY DO YOU GRASP INFORMATION?

Think about how you learn, because how you learn is most likely how you teach. If it takes you awhile to understand directions or new procedures, you most likely empathize with clients who need a little extra time from you to explain what you want them to do. This approach may annoy a client who easily grasps the picture and resents your explaining it over and over again.

HOW TALKATIVE ARE YOU?

Do you talk to people everywhere you go? If you are very talkative, you may frustrate the client who wants you to get to the point. The reverse may be also true: the client who wants to talk about everything and not concentrate on your message may frustrate you.

ARE YOU A MORNING OR A NIGHT PERSON?

If you think best in the morning and want to have a deep conversation with a client who is a night person, both of you may become frustrated because neither of you is giving the conversation the same level of attention.

DO YOU AVOID UNPLEASANT SITUATIONS AND CONFLICTS?

You will find yourself in situations that are unpleasant. You may even have to face an aggressive client. If you feel uncomfortable in some situations, you need to practice how to use your skills to handle these situations. Certain providers sense your uncertainty and try to gain control of the situation.

DO YOU BELIEVE PEOPLE WANT TO HEAR WHAT YOU HAVE TO SAY?

Your confidence is reflected in your communication with clients. Believing in your message and in your ability to get the message across to someone else is key to effective communication.

DO YOU VOICE YOUR OPINION OR DO YOU KEEP YOUR THOUGHTS TO YOURSELF?

Your job is to assure the health and safety of children in care. If you do not normally speak up, you may find it difficult to speak up when it is necessary. Practice voicing your opinion to people with whom you feel comfortable.

DO YOU SHARE ALL YOUR THOUGHTS OR KEEP THEM TO YOURSELF?

Clients and home visitors who keep their thoughts to themselves may not be effective communicators. Clients and home visitors who talk before thinking may not communicate productively. Both of these styles can cause people to become frustrated. Learn to strike a balance between voicing your thoughts when it is important and keeping your thoughts to yourself to avoid confrontation. This is a skill that must be practiced.

DO YOU BECOME OVERWHELMED WHEN PEOPLE TALK FAST?

If you do, you need to ask some of your clients to slow down. Repeat what you are hearing to make sure you understand what is being said. If you tend to talk fast, make an effort to slow down, especially when you are explaining new information.

WHEN ANSWERING QUESTIONS, DO YOU GIVE DETAILED ANSWERS OR SHORT, POINTED ANSWERS?

Find out how your answers are perceived by the clients. Know which of them need more information and which are only looking for short answers. Then adjust your communication style as needed.

. . . .

These questions require thoughtful self-reflection to answer. If you take the time to answer them truthfully, they give you a better idea about how you communicate. Once you identify the style that best describes how you communicate, match it to the styles of the clients you visit. Conflicts are most likely to occur when you and the client have different communication styles. The following table presents potential conflicts between several communication styles and provides possible solutions.

Conflicts between Styles

In each of the following conflicts, you determine the strategy to use for better communication with your client. Determine why a conflict exists and what you need to change to communicate more effectively. Carefully examining the communication styles we've described, identifying your own style and conflicting styles will assist you in finding solutions to ineffective communication.

Home Visitor Style	Client Style	Conflict
Impatient Irma: Talks fast, makes quick decisions, is blunt and impatient	Chatty Cathy: Talkative and social, loves to joke, is very expressive	**Home Visitor:** Feels impatient and may be too blunt with the client. **Client:** Feels uncomfortable, tries to make a joke about the visit, makes the home visitor more impatient.
Chatty Cathy: Sociable, likes to joke, talks a lot about personal business	Impatient Irma: Impatient, makes quick decisions	**Home Visitor:** May take up too much time being social. **Client:** Feels impatient because home visitor takes up too much time, may respond bluntly or tactlessly, causing home visitor to become more social or make jokes to win over the client.

Home Visitor Style	Client Style	Conflict
Impatient Irma: Talks fast, is blunt and impatient, sees whole picture	Factual Fred: Needs to hear facts before making decisions	**Home Visitor:** May feel impatient with client's questions and lack of support for her ideas; may not understand that client does not see whole picture. **Client:** Feels home visitor is trying to push him into doing something he does not fully understand; may resent home visitor for not giving sufficient reasons or information. Differences may lead to frustration for the home visitor and the client.
Factual Fred: Looks at all facts, is detail oriented	Impatient Irma: Sees big picture, makes quick decisions, is poor listener	**Home Visitor:** Tries to present all facts and details about topic or goal. **Client:** May become impatient because she quickly grasps big picture and understands what home visitor is trying to communicate; direct conflict between these two communication styles leads to frustration and breakdown in communication on both sides.
Agreeable Annie: Avoids conflict, wants people to like her, has difficulty saying no	Impatient Irma: Tactless, demanding, impatient	**Home Visitor:** Has difficulty discussing corrections or problems with client, particularly if correction involves disciplinary measures; may feel overwhelmed and unable to handle issues needing discussion, creating an argument. **Client:** May respond bluntly and tactlessly, steering conversation away from home visitor.

Home Visitor Style	Client Style	Conflict
Factual Fred: Detail-oriented, well prepared before speaking, may be perfectionist	Agreeable Annie: Introverted, avoids confrontation, does not voice her feelings	**Home Visitor:** Well prepared with details; may not recognize how client feels. **Client:** May not agree with home visitor; nods her head in agreement to avoid confrontation. Home visitor's perfectionism can make client feel inadequate. Home visitor and client miss opportunities to identify problems and reach resolutions.

Listening Skills

When you think back to a visit, you may be most concerned with whether or not the client heard what you had to say or if you heard what she had to say. Listening and hearing are different concepts. You may hear people talking in the next booth at a restaurant. Although you can physically hear the sounds, unless your brain is registering the words and the meaning of the words, you are not really listening. Effective listening requires more than simply hearing. Good listening takes preparation and practice. And it is worth it! Listening involves connecting with a client and making her feel comfortable.

A home visitor may not listen effectively for many reasons. Often you have more than one duty to perform during the visit. Your job may include monitoring a provider's home child care environment to assure that she is adhering to regulations and that the children are safe. You may be addressing a complaint or a noncompliance issue. These are very powerful and weighty responsibilities. Nonetheless, you must ensure that your message does not become more important than what the client has to say. Make sure you do not do all the talking. Give her a chance to speak. Your goal is to make sure she understands your instructions and is going to implement them. Listening skills are important to achieve this goal.

Avoid giving the impression you do not value what the client has to say. Evaluate yourself and keep the following in mind:

- Do not look at your watch or the door when the client is speaking.
- Do not continually interrupt the client with your opinion.
- Do not avoid eye contact.
- Do not fidget or play with your paperwork while the client is speaking.
- Do not make inappropriate facial expressions.
- Do not pay more attention to what you are going to say next than to listening to what she is saying.

Use your listening skills. Make sure you give your undivided attention to the client when she is speaking. Do not think about how you are going to counter her argument. Remember that one way to retain clients is to make them feel respected and worthy. Listening carefully does this.

Listening to clients and giving them a chance to speak does not mean you agree with them. Acknowledging their point of view shows them respect and support and helps build a relationship in which differences can be openly discussed.

Listening can be especially difficult when clients complain about a disservice or injustice they feel has been done to them. When you have heard the complaint many times, it may be difficult to listen again. But you must. Listening carefully to what the client says can help you determine what she wants. She may be venting and complaining while at bottom she wants something to change. Try to discern what she is really asking for. To do so, you must ask questions and give her your undivided attention. Ask questions that draw out the client's feelings. For example, do not ask her, "Why do you feel that way?" A "why" question can put her on the defensive. Instead, ask, "When did you start to feel this way?" or "What bothers you the most about this situation?" Acknowledge her answers with good eye contact. Lean forward, do not interrupt, and occasionally nod your head to show you are listening.

Do not always give your opinion. A client may be upset over something that in your opinion is trivial, but recognize that the problem is not trivial to her. Resist saying, "I don't think you should let that bother you." Instead, ask, "How do you feel about . . . ?"

Taking the time to identify and validate the client's feelings is called active listening. Use this skill to make sure you fully and clearly understand what she is saying. The key to successful active listening is sincere interest in understanding what the other person is feeling. If your goal is to understand her feelings, you must concentrate on what she is saying and make sure you understand it before you speak.

You may feel the client is saying one thing to you, and yet the next minute she is saying something else. To alleviate any misunderstanding or confusion, restate what you have heard: "To make sure I am understanding you correctly, I hear you saying . . ." Rephrase and paraphrase. Do not add your own opinions or concerns. Listen and verify your perception of what the client is telling you.

Once you have defined and clarified the problem she is describing, try to identify the feelings she is expressing. This can be done by saying, "*You* feel (identify the feeling) because (state the action)." For example, "*You* feel angry when I drop in unannounced because *you* do not have your paperwork up to date." If you are unsure of the provider's underlying issue, ask more probing questions to understand what she is really saying. For example, "I would like to understand more about why you feel the way you do. Are you having a problem scheduling the time to do your paperwork, or is there something about the paperwork that confuses you?"

Before the two of you can come to an agreeable solution, the client must also understand your perspective. Using "I messages" is a good way to help her understand your perspective without becoming confrontational. You can let her know you have listened to what she has said and that the situation affects you differently. "I messages" do not place blame. They create an atmosphere for problem solving and positive communication. "I messages" have three parts:

1. I feel (state the feeling): "I feel discouraged . . ."
2. When you (state the other person's behavior): ". . .when you are so angry."
3. I want (state what you want to happen): "I want to help you develop a schedule that allows you to complete your paperwork daily."

Examine the difference between using the above "I message" and saying this: "You make me discouraged because you never have your paperwork done when I visit. You know it needs to be completed on a daily basis." Notice how using "I messages" takes the confrontation out of the communication.

Once you let the client know that you understand her problem, and she understands yours, you can work together toward a solution to the problem. Understanding each other's position and respecting each side of the issue often leads to finding a middle ground that is agreeable and workable for both of you.

Nonverbal Communication and Body Language

Every time you communicate with another person, you encounter nonverbal communication in the form of body language. What people feel inside is often reflected in how they move, their facial expressions, how they stand, even their subtle gestures. In some cases, body language can convey your entire message. For example, simply raising your hand, palm facing outward, means "stop." Nodding your head can mean "yes."

As a home visitor, you may encounter times when the client is saying yes with her words but her body language is saying no. Developing an understanding of these signals will help you become aware of how she is really feeling. This can help you communicate your message more effectively. Learning to understand body language will also help you become more aware of how you communicate your own messages.

The study of body language is very complex. Many researchers have studied the subtle signs of personal display for years. Researchers have determined that words account for only 7 percent of our communication, whereas tone of voice (38 percent) and body language (55 percent) account for the majority of our communication. Other researchers have found that humans can produce up to 700,000 different body signals reflected by body position and actions, 250,000 facial expressions, and 5,000 distinct hand gestures (Phipps 2008).

One of the difficult tasks you are asked to carry out is conveying to a client her need to change a particular behavior. This may be a regulatory, safety, documentation, or other issue with consequences to the client if she fails to make necessary changes. Often your request causes the client to become defensive. Once she becomes defensive, she will not listen to your message. Instead, she will be concentrating on formulating her defense. Signs that clients are defensive include these cues:

- Turning her body away from you
- Looking down
- Crossing her arms
- Showing little facial expression
- Clenching her hands

You also need to pay attention to your own body language to ensure that you are not exhibiting signs of defensiveness. Body language that is receptive, open, and comfortable helps put the client at ease, making her more receptive to your message. Carefully watch her reaction to what you are saying. If the conversation seems to be turning negative, check your body language, tone of voice, facial expression, and eye contact. Receptive body language includes the following:

- Eye contact
- Hands relaxed, in your lap or open on the table
- Body facing the provider and tilting slightly toward her
- Relaxed facial expression, smile

Occasionally you may need to determine if a client is telling the truth or lying. Some of the signs of lying are also signs of defensiveness or nervousness. Because each person is different, do not use these signs as conclusive evidence that a person is lying. Rather, if you notice these signs, they should raise your awareness that the client may not be receptive or truthful. When you observe these behaviors, probe a little more deeply to determine if she is indeed lying. The following are common body language cues to look for when trying to determine if a person is lying:

- No eye contact; looks from side to side but does not establish eye contact
- Body turned away
- Touches the nose
- Increased perspiration
- Red in the face and neck, breathes rapidly
- Clears throat
- Changes pitch of voice

Body language can mean different things in various cultures and ethnic groups. You should never jump to conclusions when interpreting body language, especially when you are just beginning to learn to recognize nonverbal cues. Asking more questions and probing more deeply may validate your interpretations. Think about what you know about a client's personality. She may feel more comfortable when she crosses her arms, for example. Women often cross their arms when they are cold. Before you label a person aggressive or defensive, watch her natural habits and mannerisms while you are talking to her about a nonconfrontational issue, because doing so helps establish a baseline. For example, one client may always stand with arms crossed; another may touch her ears and chin or play with her hair, even when she is comfortable. Learning these natural mannerisms helps you interpret client's body language.

Learning to understand body language takes a lot of practice. When you can sit back and watch people, take advantage of it. Try to identify some subtle and nonsubtle actions and reactions. Look for the way a client positions her head. Watch the movement of her eyes, hands, feet and legs, and how she places her body. Many nonverbal behaviors are revealed through certain body language signs:

Aggression	• Placing hands on hips • Pointing finger	**Indecision**	• Pulling at ear
Apprehension	• Clasping hands behind the back • Locking ankles	**Being judgmental**	• Hand-to-face gesturing • Tilting head • Peering over glasses • Putting hand to bridge of nose
Boredom	• Doodling • Drumming fingers on surface • Crossing legs, kicking foot • Resting head in palms of hands • Staring blankly	**Lying, suspicion***	• Clearing throat • Coughing • Avoiding eye contact • Glancing sideways • Rubbing eyes
Defensiveness	• Folding arms across chest • Looking down • Clenching hands • Body turned away • Turning palms down	**Receptiveness**	• Leaning forward, uncrossing legs • Relaxing facial expression, smiling • Opening hands and arms, palms up
Defiance	• Narrowing eyes	**Rejection**	• Touching nose • Reducing eye contact
Disagreement	• Picking imaginary lint off clothing		
Discomfort	• Fidgeting • Playing with hair or jewelry		
Frustration	• Breathing shallowly • Clenching hands tightly • Wringing hands • Running hand through hair • Rubbing back of neck • Kicking at ground		

*Do not accuse a person of lying simply because you observe some of these gestures. Nonetheless, they offer some clues to prompt more questions and to probe more deeply into miscommunications.

CHECKPOINT—Communication

Learning effective communication skills takes practice and self-examination. If a visit goes wrong, do not automatically blame the client. It is your responsibility to accommodate your style to the client's. You should not expect her to accommodate hers to yours. After each home visit, both negative and positive, ask yourself the following questions:

- How well did you communicate on this visit?
- What did you do to facilitate the communication positively?
- What did you do that affected the communication negatively?
- How could you have conducted this visit differently?

Be Assertive

Module Description

It is the home visitor's job to assure that the providers' services meet certain standards, regulatory requirements, and contractual obligations. You do this in a number of ways: You conduct home visits that include inspections. You write corrective action plans when you find that a child care home does not meet compliance. You train providers individually and in groups.

Adequately preparing for visits in which you need to be assertive or for those in which you may have to respond to aggressive behavior is very important in carrying out your job responsibilities.

Learning Objectives

- Enhance your ability to promote negotiation while solving problems and maintaining good relationships with your clients.
- Know how to use assertive language and assertive listening effectively.
- Communicate with authority and respect.
- Be comfortable expressing yourself and speaking up when necessary.
- Understand that there are times when saying no is important.

· · · · · · · · ·

Case Study

· ·

Last month, when Ida visited Rosa, she found that Rosa was having landscaping work done in her yard. To get the large equipment into the yard, the workers had removed a portion of Rosa's fence. As a provider, Rosa was required to have a fence because railroad tracks lay just beyond her yard. Rosa assured Ida the fence was going to be fixed immediately; in the meantime, she would not let the children play in the yard.

Yesterday Ida drove by Rosa's home and noticed that the section of fence had not been put back in place. She did not see any children outside. Ida decides she needs to make an unannounced visit to Rosa and be more assertive in her request to fix the fence.

In preparing for her visit to Rosa, Ida first identifies the action she wants Rosa to take. Rosa clearly needs to fix the fence immediately. Next Ida thinks about Rosa's personality. She knows Rosa is chatty, likes to make jokes, and often does not take Ida seriously. Ida also knows that as happy as Rosa can be, she also can become very emotional when upset. Ida realizes she is going to have to clearly identify the goal and stick to the subject—fixing the fence.

Then Ida looks at Rosa's file. She finds that Rosa has been cited in the past for not having a gate closed at the top of the stairs. Rosa corrected the problem immediately. She also notes that Rosa has been cited for being overenrolled on one occasion, and again Rosa corrected the problem immediately. Rosa's lack of compliance worries Ida and strengthens her resolve to make the visit.

Ida researches the regulation for fencing, and she copies Rosa's child care license, which specifically states that the yard must be fenced in. She wants to make sure she has all supporting documents with her.

As she thinks about the visit, Ida knows her facial expressions must convey the importance of the goal. Ida knows this might be difficult because Rosa deals with problems by joking and does not like to take things seriously. Ida will have to make Rosa see the seriousness of this problem.

Ida thinks about how she will present the noncompliance to Rosa. She does not want to begin with accusatory language, such as "You have not fixed the fence." Ida knows this will put Rosa on the defensive immediately. She decides the best way to approach the problem will be to state it impersonally and simply state the fact: "The fence needs to be repaired immediately."

Ida prepares to use her assertive skill to solve the problem. She plans on being direct and respectful, and she hopes to maintain her good relationship with Rosa.

The next day is a beautiful warm day, and as Ida drives up to Rosa's house, she sees all six of Rosa's preschool children playing in the yard. Ida knows she is going to have to tell Rosa to take the children inside. For a moment Ida, is reluctant to confront Rosa. Ida has learned how to be assertive, but she has a naturally passive personality. She likes to make people happy, and she does not like confrontation. Ida also knows that if she does not immediately address the noncompliance problem, she will jeopardize her working relationship with Rosa and possibly the children's well-being. She must assert herself. She takes a deep breath and gets out of the car.

As Ida walks into the yard, Rosa greets her with a big smile, comments on the beautiful day, and proceeds to relay a funny comment one of the children made. Rosa completely ignores the fact that the fence is not repaired.

Ida laughs at Rosa's story and agrees it is a beautiful day. Ida then tells Rosa the fence needs to be repaired immediately. Rosa laughs and says, "Oh, you noticed that!" Ida does not laugh; she tells Rosa that the children cannot play in the yard until the fence is up. Rosa laughs and says, "I am planning on having it fixed this weekend." She continues in a laughing way, "You aren't really going to tell these children they have to go inside on such a beautiful day?"

Ida realizes this is an important moment in the conversation. She knows she must draw on her assertive skills. She also knows Rosa needs a lot of encouragement. Ida says, "Let's take the children into the house and talk about it." Rosa understands by Ida's facial expression and tone of voice that she is serious.

After the children are inside and settled at the table with a snack, Ida brings out the fencing regulations. Before Ida can say anything, Rosa says, "It has been rainy the last few weeks, so I was not able to have the fence fixed. I didn't want to keep the children inside." Rosa is beginning to get angry. She states, "I was watching the children really carefully." Ida recognizes that Rosa is making excuses. Ida respectfully listens to Rosa without commenting or making judgmental statements. When Rosa is finished, Ida wants Rosa to know she understands, so she says, "I understand you have tried to fix the fence and the weather has not cooperated. I can also understand not wanting to keep the children in on such a beautiful day." After letting Rosa know she understands her point of view,

Ida uses her constructive feedback skills by clearly stating the problem and what needs to be done to correct it. By responding in this assertive way, Ida gets the point across to Rosa without angering or humiliating her. Rosa knows what she needs to do. She says, "I understand, and I am going to see if I can get someone in today to fix the fence. In the meantime, I will have to keep the children out of the yard."

Ida tells Rosa she will stop by the next day. She commends her on her decision to take care of the problem immediately. Ida is glad she has used her assertive skills to effectively convey the importance of her message to Rosa. As Ida leaves Rosa's house, she feels confident that the fence will be fixed and the children will be a safe.

· · · · · · · · · ·

Assertiveness

Assertiveness is a skill that all home visitors need to develop. You are asked to go into providers' homes to inspect, determine compliance, and assess the services provided. If those services do not meet contractual or regulatory standards, you need to use the assertive skills presented in this module. Of course, your first priority must always be the safety and well-being of the children in care. You may have to require immediate correction when unsafe conditions exist.

Before discussing assertive behavior and skills, it's important to know the difference between the words *assertive* and *aggressive*. According to *Encarta World English Dictionary* (2009), an assertive person behaves confidently and persistently in stating a position or a claim. An aggressive person is someone who shows a readiness or has a tendency to attack or do harm to others. Examine some more specific differences here.

Assertive Behavior
- Promotes negotiation
- Promotes problem solving
- Promotes good relationships
- Is direct and respectful
- Is a win/win approach
- Is goal oriented
- Promotes trust

Aggressive Behavior
- Promotes anger
- Promotes negative consequences
- Makes demands
- Is direct and tactless
- Is a win/lose approach
- Is controlling
- Promotes resentment

Assertive behavior promotes positive relationships by taking the feelings of others into consideration. Aggressive behavior, on the other hand, may solve the problem but promotes feelings of humiliation and resentment. It should never be viewed as successful.

Walking the fine line between assertive and aggressive behavior can be difficult. Home visitors may feel quite unpopular when discipline or corrective action needs to be taken. People feel more confident in their own environment, and since your home visits take place in the provider's own home, you may start at a disadvantage. If a provider anticipates your visit and becomes defensive, she may overreact, aggressively and emotionally confronting you before you are prepared for it. When a provider acts aggressively, do not take it personally. Remember that she is probably angry at the situation, not at you.

If you anticipate a negative reaction while going into a tough situation, you may come across negatively from the beginning. Your attitude will set the tone for the whole visit. You can help set a cooperative and positive tone by examining your own comfort with assertiveness. Know your personality. Which description below best fits you?

- Passive: You don't feel you have the right to be heard. You often feel uncomfortable expressing yourself, fearful that you will not like the response you receive. You are usually willing to back down easily to avoid conflict.
- Assertive: You are comfortable expressing what you think. You can express your views without stepping on others, without anger or attack. Your goal is to find a resolution that works for everyone.
- Aggressive: You stand up for yourself, even at the expense of others. You use tactics like a loud voice, sarcasm, and forcefulness to get your way.

Step back and think about your personality. When using aggression, you may feel satisfied that you've achieved your goal. You need to think about how the client is feeling; using aggressive tactics makes the client feel uncomfortable, angry, or intimidated. Instead of focusing on the importance of your message, the client is probably concentrating on her own hurt feelings. Accomplish your goals without intimidation. Do not leave a client with hurt feelings.

Prepare to Be Assertive

Good preparation for home visits includes knowing what you want to accomplish. Clearly define your objectives. You cannot predict how the provider will react to your visit, so you must be prepared for a variety of outcomes and perspectives. Prepare your response to the different reactions you can anticipate. Put thought into the mutual goals for yourself and your client, and prepare how to present those goals. The case study demonstrates how Ida's planning helped her keep her objectives clear and feel more confident.

Part of your preparation should include examining your past history with the client. Ask yourself the following questions:

- Is the provider chronically out of compliance?
- Does the provider try to make you responsible for the solution?
- What is the history of the severity of her noncompliance?

Asking yourself these questions will help you develop your strategy for addressing problems. For example, Ida was concerned about Rosa's previous citations and knew she should use all possible tools to convince Rosa of the seriousness of the fencing problem. Continue your preparation by examining the following points.

Assertive individuals try to understand others and acknowledge the value that others bring to situations. In a conflict, assertive people listen actively, explain themselves clearly, and invite others to work with them toward a solution. Assertive people recognize that to have successful working relationships with others, they must not create barriers with anger or humiliation.

Documentation

Make sure you have all the documentation and paperwork you need to support your position. Show the provider the documentation and remind her in a concerned manner that she has contractual obligations and responsibilities.

Have you ever heard, "But I didn't know you wanted me to . . ."? Occasionally misunderstandings can occur. The client may have misinterpreted previous concerns or requests you have expressed. Be aware, however, that she may also use what you perceive as a misunderstanding as an excuse for not correcting a noncompliance. Therefore, you must document your visit, making sure to include the date, time, outcome, what action is expected and when, and any additional information about your attempts to correct a noncompliance. You and the client should sign the documentation, and a copy should be given to her. This documentation can be used to ensure there are no misunderstandings.

Eye Contact

Direct eye contact uses body language to state that you need to be listened to. Avoid staring and glaring, which are aggressive behaviors. Achieving the appropriate amount of eye contact takes practice. When you engage in direct eye contact, occasionally look away so that you don't make the client uncomfortable. Looking away periodically does not mean you avoid her eyes altogether. If you avoid her eyes and look down, you convey that you are uncomfortable with your message. Similarly, looking past the client to the door or to the side conveys the message that you really do not want to be there. One solution is to occasionally glance at the papers in your hands or at paperwork on the table.

Facial Expressions and Body Language

Make sure your facial expression and body language fit the message you are attempting to convey. Try to keep your expression relaxed. Do not lean toward the client; this is an aggressive stance. Try to be at her same level. For example, if she is sitting down and you are standing, she may feel that you are looking down on her. Try to remain at eye level with your client. Be respectful of her personal space. Always be mindful of keeping a comfortable distance and not crowding her. Do not fidget. Relax your body as much as you can. For more about body language, see module 5.

Tone of Voice

Pay attention to the tone of your voice. Make sure it is not angry, overly loud, patronizing, or too soft. Often when people are nervous, they speak too fast. Practice what you want to say so that you can control how your message is delivered. Be careful not to raise your voice at the end of a statement. This makes you sound as if you are uncertain and are asking a question instead of making a statement.

Clear Language

Know in advance what your objectives are. State them in clear, understandable language. Do not use words, abbreviations, or phrases that may be unfamiliar to the client. Organize your presentation. Concentrate on making the objective rather than the client the target of your conversation.

Listen

Allow the client time to state her opinion. This shows respect. While acknowledging her right to feel the way she does, you should remain firm—especially when your objective concerns a regulatory or contractual issue. For more about listening, see module 5.

Use Assertive Language

When you want to be assertive, what you say and how you say it determines how well your message is conveyed. You need to make sure that your message concentrates on goals and not on the client's faults. Don't think of being assertive during home visits as winning or losing. Instead, look at it as a way to negotiate a solution to problems or situations. Establish a common goal and work with your client to accomplish that goal. Listening to her thoughts and feelings will help you build a workable relationship. Remember, even though you may be in the position to enforce regulations, you and she are a team working toward a common goal. Do not start a discussion with "You," "You never," or "You always." These terms are likely to put the client on the defensive immediately.

Words like *never* and *always* set you up for debate and argument. When you use such generalizations, you shift the focus away from your objective. The client tries to defend herself by coming up with counterexamples, and the focus moves to accusations and defenses. When a client can refute your generalizations, she weakens your position and strengthens hers. Keep your statements fact-based. For example, if you say to the client, "You never have your paperwork in on time," she responds with "That's not true. I got my paperwork in on time in February." Her focus is now on defending herself and proving you wrong.

An important goal for you is promoting feelings of cooperation and teamwork. Using words like *we, our,* and *us* conveys the message that the objective is mutual and that achieving it is in the best interest of both parties. Often it is better to remove the pronouns from your sentence altogether. Now you are putting the focus on the action or situation needing attention. For example, you say, "The attendance forms must be submitted by the fifth of the month to receive the reimbursement check on time."

The following scenario and outcomes provide additional ideas for applying these language skills.

Scenario

You go into a home and notice a baby whose crib has a cord hanging next to it. This is an unsafe situation. The baby could grab the cord and become wrapped up in it or pull down the attached object, resulting in injury or even death. This unsafe violation of licensing regulations *must* be corrected immediately.

OPTION 1

You say, "You need to do something about that cord immediately!"

OUTCOME 1

People do not react well to demands. Remember, you are in the provider's home, and you are now criticizing her environment, judgment, and ability to keep children safe. She is likely to become defensive.

OPTION 2

You say, "We need to do something about that cord immediately!"

OUTCOME 2

Even though you are using "we," in this situation, the provider may still perceive the statement as a demand and become defensive.

OPTION 3

You say, "That cord is too close to the crib. Let's move the crib or move the cord."

OUTCOME 3

Here you are stating the problem and sharing in the solution without criticizing the provider. You are focusing on the action that must be taken, not on the person.

Assertive Listening

Part of being assertive is listening well to another person. Let your client know that you want to understand her point of view. Remember, understanding is different from agreeing. You can understand what she is saying and still disagree with her. Let her know you are interested in hearing and understanding her point of view. You can accomplish this in several steps.

Have you ever had a discussion with someone who was obviously not paying attention to what you were saying? It's frustrating to feel that the person you are talking to does not value what you have to say. If you use assertive listening skills, you will never make a client feel this way. You will listen, really listen, to what she is saying.

1. Concentrate: This type of listening begins with concentration. Often in a stressful or emotionally charged situation, you can find it hard to concentrate because your thoughts may are racing.

2. Relax: Try to gain your composure and relax. This is not always easy; you may need to excuse yourself and go to your car until you feel ready to concentrate.

3. Check your body language: When listening, remember how important body language can be. If you are tense, tapping your foot, or sitting in a rigid manner, the client may mirror your body language. Try to sit or stand in a relaxed way. Lean toward her, showing that you are listening. Occasionally nod your head. Displaying an open posture encourages the client to speak.

4. Ask questions: After listening, tell the client what you have understood her to say. If she does not agree, ask questions. Encourage her to voice her thoughts, opinions, and feelings. If you still do not understand her point of view, tell her you are confused and ask her to clarify for you. Continue to tell her that you may be coming from a different perspective, but you are interested in her thoughts on the situation.

5. Establish mutual respect: When you validate a client's response respectfully, she may be more receptive to hearing your point of view. Establishing this level of mutual respect will be helpful throughout your relationship.

Respond to Passive-Aggressive Behavior

Some people exhibit passive-aggressive behaviors. A passive-aggressive behavior includes smiles and ready agreement to your request, seeming enthusiasm about your suggestions, but contradictory actions. Passive-aggressive behavior may include procrastination or failures to carry out your request effectively. Such actions may result in the opposite of what you requested. You see this behavior when working with a client who agrees with what you ask her to do, but when you return, you find that she has done nothing about carrying out your request. Clients have plenty of reasons for not carrying out your request. Passive-aggressive behavior includes the following excuses.

- I tried, but I don't know how to do it.
- I meant to do it, but I forgot.
- It's not my fault because (someone or some situation kept me from carrying out the request).
- I was going to do it next week.
- It's not fair! I don't know why they (authority) want me to do this, anyway.
- I can't.

Passive-aggressive behavior offers excuses and sometimes triggers your own guilt for having made a request.

For example, a provider says, "I know I told you I would clean up the car parts in the children's play area, but my husband promised to help me and he hasn't had time. I know you don't want me to make my husband angry." Her explanation not only excuses her own responsibility; it also assigns responsibility to you for angering her husband.

When you identify a client who is behaving passively-aggressively, you have some positive options. Ask questions after you have made your request so she must give you feedback on how she is really feeling:

- What do you think your first step should be?
- What information do you need to fully understand what is required?
- How do you feel about making the necessary changes?

When you ask a question, give the client time to answer. Listen carefully to her answer. Even if she is behaving negatively and complaining, you need to listen respectfully. After you have heard her comments, excuses, or complaints, do not respond in a demeaning or a sarcastic manner. Remember to control your body language. If you roll your eyes or cross your arms, you send a negative and disapproving message. Instead, acknowledge what you have heard. You might say, "I understand how you are feeling." Or you might ask more questions.

Once you have listened and understood her, restate what and why it is necessary for her to be responsible for making the change. Do not allow her to manipulate you into taking responsibility for making the correction. Do not do the work for her. Clearly define your own and her respective responsibilities. Read the following example to see how assertiveness skills can be used effectively in dealing with passive-aggressive behavior.

You enter a provider's home and observe the same unsanitary conditions that were present during a past visit. You say, "During our previous visit, we discussed ways you would keep debris from collecting on the kitchen floor. I am surprised to see that the floor still looks unsanitary."

You listen to the provider's feedback. You remain neutral while she whines and makes excuses. Then you say, "I know you want what is best for the children in your program. I also know you understand there are regulatory requirements about sanitation. Let's come up with a workable solution so that when I visit again, I can document how you've improved your maintenance."

By responding in an assertive way, you get your point across without angering or humiliating your client. Had you used passive behavior, the provider might have continued to ignore the requirements for good sanitation. If you had employed an aggressive approach, the provider might have lost sight of your point in an angry exchange.

Practice the assertive skills discussed in this chapter. Employing them gives you the best chance to deliver your message successfully. If you have other home visitors with whom you can role-play different scenarios, do so. Use the checklist that follows after you have completed actual visits to help you identify your strengths and weaknesses. Doing so gives you an opportunity to think about what you could have done differently.

 CHECKPOINT—Your Assertiveness Skills

After completing a difficult visit, use the following checklist to evaluate how well you applied your assertiveness skills:

- Did you feel comfortable using your assertive skills?

- Were you able to negotiate a solution to the problem?

- How well did you use assertive language? What words in particular did you use to promote cooperation?

- Did you give constructive feedback?

- Did the client exhibit an emotion you were not prepared to address?

- Did you understand the client's point of view?

- How did you let the client know you understood?

- Do you feel comfortable with the resolution?

- Did you document your visit?

- Would you have said or done anything differently? If so, what?

Module 7

Motivate Yourself and Others

Module Description

An important part of a home visitor's job is to bring training and technical assistance into a provider's home. For example, you can bring the knowledge of best practices in health and safety, curriculum, and child development to the providers you visit. This module discusses how you can motivate providers to adopt any changes you recommend.

Motivation means to move a person to develop or to stop a behavior. There's the saying, "You can lead a horse to water, but you can't make it drink"—the same is true about providers. You can lead providers to best practices, but you can't make them adopt them. How many times have you been frustrated after spending many hours training providers to adopt a new skill or practice, only to find they are not applying what you have taught them? Motivation bridges the gap between knowing something and wanting to apply it. Motivation supplies the need or the reason why a person adopts a certain behavior.

To motivate providers, you need to know what causes resistance and how to overcome it. This module discusses the types of motivation and what works best for your clients. It will furnish you with the skills to motivate providers to adopt the best practices you introduce.

This module also addresses your own motivation. Because you are in the position of motivating others, you must maintain your own motivation to reach the goals you set for yourself and for your clients.

Learning Objectives

- Recognize that change can be hard for some clients.
- Be aware of cultural differences.
- Understand the importance of intrinsic motivation and how to instill it in your clients.
- Establish short-term and long-term goals for clients and follow up on them.
- Know where to find support for yourself.
- Set goals for yourself.

. . . .

Case Study

Carmen has been a home visitor for three years. In looking at her list of clients, she realizes that although many of them have set and reached goals to improve the quality of care they give to children, some have not adopted any of the best practices she has been teaching. She decides to concentrate her efforts on the providers who do not seem to be motivated.

The first provider she chooses is Keisha. Keisha has been a provider for twelve years and is reluctant to make any changes in the way she operates her child care. She rarely attends trainings, and when Carmen attempts to show her something new, she expresses the feeling that she doesn't see why she should change. For example, Carmen has been trying to motivate Keisha to develop a curriculum for the children who come to her facility after school. Carmen is concerned, because when she visits Keisha during after-school hours, she often observes the school-age children seated in front of the TV, watching a movie.

Carmen knows Keisha's personality; she knows she must carefully develop a plan before presenting it to Keisha. Carmen also knows Keisha can be a perfectionist and will not make quick decisions. To motivate Keisha, Carmen gathers some handouts and facts on best practices in after-school care. Carmen knows she must help Keisha see the value of developing a school-age curriculum.

On her next trip to Keisha's, Carmen visits during naptime so she can sit and talk undisturbed with Keisha. As soon as they are seated, Carmen enthusiastically tells Keisha she has some very interesting information to show her. She shows Keisha the printed handouts and presents her with facts on the benefits of good after-school care. She also demonstrates to Keisha how a good schedule can make her day run more smoothly. Keisha reads the handouts. Her first response is to tell Carmen that the children like to watch TV and that she really does not have the time to develop an after-school curriculum.

Carmen begins to feel discouraged. She has put a lot of time into gathering information for Keisha. She decides to draw on her motivational skills and keep trying. Carmen realizes that the goal of creating an after-school curriculum may sound daunting. She also realizes that Keisha may not have the confidence to develop a curriculum. Knowing that Keisha is a perfectionist, Carmen decides to break down the goal into small, attainable steps. She thinks about the materials she has brought.

She remembers that she has printed out specific instructions for some easy after-school activities. One involves the children making a fruit dip for their snack. Carmen presents this activity to Keisha. Carmen shows her the concepts the children would be learning during this cooking activity. Keisha hasn't realized how one cooking activity could contain so many areas of learning for the children. She agrees to try the activity.

The next week, Carmen drops in on Keisha. Keisha is excited to tell her how enthusiastic the children are about the activity. All of the children, including the younger ones, loved the nutritious dip. Carmen praises Keisha for accomplishing such a successful activity. Keisha expresses how pleased she felt watching the children enjoy themselves, all the while knowing she was giving the school-age children opportunities to develop new skills. Keisha also tells Carmen that while she was supervising the older children in cooking, she had the younger children searching through old magazines to find pictures of fruit. Later the older children helped the younger ones make a collage. Keisha says how satisfied she was to see the older children helping the younger ones. Carmen praises Keisha for being so creative. She then turns to the school-age children and asks them how they liked the cooking activity. The children are all talking and smiling at once as they express their enjoyment. Carmen looks at Keisha. She sees her beaming as she hears the positive feedback from the children. Carmen then brainstorms with Keisha on other activities to add to Keisha's curriculum.

As Carmen leaves Keisha's house, she feels very pleased by the enthusiasm she has seen in Keisha. She congratulates herself for a successful visit. She now feels motivated to develop a plan for the next reluctant provider on her list.

• • • • • • • •

Motivate Clients

An important part of your work as a home visitor is to motivate providers to accept the best practices you teach. Motivating means that you must find a way to present reasons and encouragement to move a provider toward learning a skill or knowledge of a specific subject. Motivating also involves providing incentives. In an ideal situation, you would be able to offer incentives to satisfy each provider's feelings of self-worth and dignity and form a partnership based on mutual respect. In reality, many of the regulations and documentation requirements change constantly. As more and more documentation is required of you, more is also expected of providers.

In this climate, you may find it increasingly difficult to foster feelings of partnership, since you are always introducing more requirements that need to be met. You may be viewed as the demanding boss, someone who is never satisfied with what the provider does. Your goals may be seen as determined by the quality of the paperwork rather than the quality of the child care. Your visits may be viewed as unpleasant intrusions in the provider's schedule instead of welcomed visits providing positive feedback and rewards.

How can you successfully regulate providers using a motivational approach? We begin by examining some of the reasons clients resist learning new things.

Busy Schedule

Family child care providers care for multiage children. They must integrate activities and developmentally appropriate practices for several ages. Their family responsibilities also demand their attention. Adding a new obligation or task to their already busy schedule can overwhelm some providers.

Resistance to Change

Some providers have been in the child care business for many years. They have consistently run successful child care programs in which the children are safe and happy. They do not see the need to learn anything new or to change any of their procedures.

Low Self-Esteem

Some providers feel incapable of learning a new skill or procedure. They doubt that they can successfully apply new learning to their child care. Their attitude, therefore, is *Why even try?*

Negative Feelings

Other providers may feel they are not being paid enough to use their time to go to a training or to implement a new skill.

. . . .

Knowing why providers are not presently motivated to learn is a first step in understanding how to motivate them. Carefully review the suggestions and strategies presented in this module to help clients overcome any resistance they might have to learning and to motivate them to approach learning eagerly and enthusiastically.

Extrinsic Motivation

Extrinsic motivation comes from outside. It is positive when it is praise or comes in the form of things like money, awards, or certificates. Extrinsic motivation can also be negative, as in punishment or discipline. Extrinsic motivation usually drives a person toward a goal that is required by someone else. Often the motivation wanes unless the positive or negative incentive is regularly increased or intensified. If the incentive is removed, the motivation usually stops.

John Shindler, author of *Transformative Classroom Management* (2009), is one of many experts who believes that extrinsic motivators may actually decrease motivation. These experts believe that extrinsic motivation may only motivate people to make changes when they are forced to, not because they believe changes are best. If a person is only performing an activity for the external reward, she may fail to appreciate or even recognize any intrinsic rewards (see below for a discussion of intrinsic rewards). If the external reward is removed, will the person still be motivated to use the behavior that has been rewarded?

It's true that providers set goals to obtain extrinsic rewards. For example, in many states, providers need to attend training for a certain number of hours to obtain and renew a child care license. Often a provider attends only enough trainings to meet her hourly requirement. Her extrinsic reward is attainment or renewal of her license.

Extrinsic rewards may extend beyond mandated compliance. A provider may take training because it benefits another area of her life. For example, she needs to fill the last slot in her child care, and the only child available at the moment has severe allergies. Before she can take the child, she must learn how to use an auto-injector of epinephrine (such as EpiPen Jr or Twinject). The provider may take the training because she is motivated by the additional income she will receive after enrolling the child in her care. Another provider wants to learn the universal precautions used to decrease the spread of HIV/AIDS. Her motivation is extrinsic because her reward is knowing she is protecting herself and the children in her care from the disease.

Extrinsic rewards also come in the form of recognition. Some providers may be very competitive; they need to know they have excelled. For example, a provider may be motivated to send attendance forms in on time because an organization with which she is affiliated awards providers who have a perfect record of sending in their attendance forms on time. Some providers desire things like a certificate or an acknowledgment in the child care system's newspaper.

Intrinsic Motivation

Intrinsic motivation comes from inside. It is usually driven by a person's desire to meet a goal. When a provider is intrinsically motivated, she wants to do the right thing. Her feelings include self-esteem and satisfaction. The American psychologist Abraham Maslow spent much of his time researching human motivation. He developed a hierarchy of human needs that he believed motivate people to action:

1. The need to satisfy physical needs (for example, food, shelter, and water)
2. The need to feel safe and secure
3. The need to feel loved and accepted
4. The need to achieve, feel competent, and gain approval and recognition
5. The need to be self-aware and fulfill one's potential

Maslow's hierarchy contends that only after the first three levels of needs are met can a person work toward the needs in level 4. When a person's efforts are recognized and they feel a sense of approval, they have reached level 4. Your goal is to help your clients reach level 5 by helping them to be aware of their potential. This self-awareness is where intrinsic motivation is achieved.

Providers spend many hours caring for children. They can become tired and feel unrewarded unless they learn to recognize moments of intrinsic satisfaction. Examples of intrinsic rewards include feeling a deep sense of satisfaction when a child attains a small goal, such as learning to verbalize feelings instead of hitting or pushing, or when a shy child becomes comfortable enough to participate in the group.

To truly motivate a provider, your goal should be to convince her to believe and accept the value of the goals set before her. Read the following example to see why intrinsic motivation is essential.

Scenario

Your state licensing regulations have been changed and a new requirement has been added. Providers are now required to conduct quarterly assessments of all preschool children in their care. Your job is to assure that these assessments are being completed.

OPTION 1

You offer the challenge with no motivation. You tell clients that this is an additional requirement that includes no monetary reward. In response to providers who complain about adding this additional activity to their schedule, you agree and commiserate with them on how unfair this added burden is.

OUTCOME 1

Providers feel burdened, used, resentful, and unmotivated to do quality assessments.

OPTION 2

You present the challenge with intrinsic motivation. You tell providers about the additional requirement, describing why it is a positive

When using intrinsic motivation with providers, here are some important points to remember:

- *Fully explain why the skill or knowledge is important to providers.*
- *Set attainable goals so providers experience success regularly.*
- *Show providers how the skill or information solves a problem for them.*

and worthwhile regulation. You demonstrate to them how the assessments will benefit them in evaluating the individual goals for each child. As an additional benefit, you demonstrate how the assessments can enhance their communication with the parents.

OUTCOME 2

Using this regulation to validate the effectiveness of providers' programs offers an intrinsic motivator that brings confirmation, pride, and recognition to providers' work.

Motivational Skills

Being an effective motivator requires good communication skills. Always listen to the provider and demonstrate that you are willing to help her learn. Intrinsic motivation needs positive recognition; therefore, make sure you do not always criticize. Remember to acknowledge and praise even the smallest progress. Your praise should include the specific accomplishment as well as the benefit to the provider and/or children she services. Don't forget to acknowledge her compliance with a regulation, even if there is disagreement with the regulation. For example, your organization may have the regulation that hot dogs cannot be fed to children under three years of age because of the choking hazard. The provider may feel that because she cuts the hot dogs up into small pieces, she is meeting the intent of the regulation. Acknowledging her attempt to comply with the intent of the regulation will be an encouraging step when motivating her to fully comply with the regulation. Let the provider know that you are helping her, and thank her for helping you carry out your job requirements.

You will know how best to motivate your client only if you actually understand what makes her tick. Each provider is unique, and you should think about how to be effective with each one:

- Consider her experience. Never talk down to her. Many providers have been in the business for many years and have valuable experience. When explaining a new requirement, acknowledge the provider's experience and build on it so she can attain the new goal. You might ask more experienced providers to mentor those who are having difficulty meeting a goal.
- Be respectful. Work with a provider in transferring new requirements into real-life situations. Work with her on her individual schedules, assisting her to see where she can implement the new requirement.

- Encourage creativity. Be open to the provider's ideas on how to reach goals. Remember that everyone does not have to do things the same way for the goal to be met successfully.
- Understand cultural differences. Be aware of cultural road blocks and address them before they become an issue.

Of course, regular self-reflection and evaluation of your interaction with the providers you visit is the best way to build on success. Carmen's actions, described in this module's case study, provide a good example of the steps involved in supporting intrinsic motivation.

Set Goals

Home visitors need to set both short- and long-term goals for providers. Carmen's long-term goal for Keisha was to implement an after-school curriculum. She broke this goal down into small units, starting with one activity. The success of that activity motivated Keisha to try additional activities. When Carmen first presented the goal, she was careful to give specific instructions on how to carry out the first activity. Keisha was not left wondering what it meant to develop a school-age curriculum. Carmen's willingness to work with Keisha and share ideas gave Keisha the confidence to go on.

Follow Up

An essential part of motivating providers is to always follow up. Carmen made an extra visit to see how Keisha did with her after-school activity. This follow-up showed Keisha the importance of conducting the activity and the importance Carmen gave it.

Remain Positive

When home visitors remain positive, they help instill confidence in the provider. From the first time she introduced the goal and at every meeting about it, Carmen was excited and enthusiastic when she discussed the goal with Keisha. She was also quick to recognize Keisha's achievement. Carmen became as enthusiastic as Keisha when she witnessed Keisha's success. She praised and encouraged Keisha.

Make It Personal

Home visitors need to accept providers' creativity. If they accomplish the intent of the goal, it doesn't matter if they have not performed the way you would have. Keisha expanded the activity Carmen had given her to all the children in her care. Carmen was pleased despite the fact that Keisha did not perform the activity exactly as she had instructed. Carmen recognized that Keisha had made the goal her own and had gone beyond what was required.

• • • • • • • • •

Carmen successfully assisted Keisha in finding internal motivation that allowed her to meet an outside goal. Carmen showed Keisha all the developmental learning domains that a single activity could address. This gave Keisha satisfaction and a feeling of self–worth that stayed with her in the form of intrinsic motivation.

Self-Motivation

Besides motivating providers, home visitors need to motivate themselves. Your job may require you to carry out disciplinary action. You may have to deal with difficult field situations. You must be responsible for all of your documentation. All of these demands can feel quite burdensome. How do you stay positive, especially at times when you are receiving negative feedback, or even retaliation, from providers? A second case study may help you with self-motivation.

Case Study

During an unannounced visit, Sarah finds that a provider, Ann, is overenrolled. Ann is licensed for large-group child care, but she must have an assistant present whenever she exceeds a certain number of children. Ann explains to Sarah that this never happens, that what Sarah is seeing is a rare situation. Ann claims that her assistant called from a doctor's office, where the doctor was running late. By the time Ann got this message from her assistant, the extra children had already arrived. She is very embarrassed and uncomfortable at being caught out of compliance with regulations.

Sarah's organization has a clear policy about this situation. If she finds that a provider is overenrolled, the provider must call parents to pick up the extra children. Sarah explains what must happen, and Ann calls one of the parents to come and pick up two of the children.

Sarah respectfully tells Ann that she is required to stay until the parent arrives. Ann seems to be growing more uncomfortable and is beginning to get angry. When the parent arrives, Sarah tells the parent she is sorry she had to ask Ann to send the children home, but because Ann's assistant didn't show up, the action was necessary in order for Ann to stay in compliance with regulations. She also reminds the parent that the policy is in place for safety reasons and that the goal is to keep her children safe. After the parent leaves, Sarah thanks Ann for her cooperation. Ann does not look at Sarah. She just shrugs her shoulders, making it obvious that she is not happy with Sarah.

After Sarah leaves, she parks her car on the next street and immediately documents what has happened at Ann's house. Back at the house, Ann becomes angrier and angrier. Rather than putting the blame on herself for the situation, she begins to think about the many ways Sarah has caused her embarrassment in front of a parent. Ann feels that Sarah's staying until the parent picked up the children implied that Sarah didn't believe she had really called the parent. Ann decides she does not want Sarah in her house again.

The next day, Ann calls Sarah's supervisor and registers a complaint against Sarah. Ann acknowledges to the supervisor that she was wrong and out of compliance. She states that she had no problem with the corrective action that needed to be taken. She goes on to say that she is extremely upset with Sarah. She feels that Sarah embarrassed her terribly in front of the parent. She also feels that Sarah treated her disrespectfully and implied that she was not being truthful.

Sarah's supervisor, Jean, arranges a meeting with Sarah to discuss the complaint. When Jean tells Sarah that Ann had called and reveals the contents of Ann's complaint, Sarah becomes angry. She has worked hard with Ann and has supported her at all times. She recalls how she helped Ann overcome difficulties with a parent.

As her anger subsides, it is replaced with discouragement. Sarah says she is thinking about quitting. She isn't happy about having to defend her actions. Sarah worries that when she enforces regulations, providers become mad at her and complain. She feels this is very unfair.

Jean attempts to calm Sarah down. She reasons with Sarah and reminds her that providers are not always going to like her or her decisions. Jean helps Sarah see that Ann is transferring the blame for her own embarrassment onto Sarah. Ann's feelings about what happened are very strong. She finds it difficult to blame herself; therefore, she blames Sarah. Sarah understands Jean's point, but she is still upset and discouraged. She believes that Jean is second-guessing how she handled the situation with Ann. Jean assures Sarah that she carried out the policy correctly and appropriately. Finally, Sarah begins to feel better. She recognizes that she did not cause the problem and that she is not responsible for how Ann feels.

Jean points out that there is still a problem that must be resolved. How will they address Ann's feelings and her request for a different home visitor? Jean directs Sarah to two possible solutions. First, she can assign Ann to another home visitor. Together they realize this will not solve the problem. Uncomfortable feelings will remain between Ann and Sarah whenever they attend meetings, trainings, or other functions together. The second solution is for Jean to accompany Sarah to Ann's house with the intention of resolving the negative feelings. Jean suggests that Sarah face Ann and let her know she did not intend to make Ann feel the way she did. At first, Sarah rebels at the idea of apologizing when she feels she did nothing wrong. Jean reasons with Sarah and helps her see that she would not be apologizing for doing her job but would simply be acknowledging her regret that Ann feels as she does. Jean and Sarah put together a plan to visit Ann in a few weeks, giving Ann the opportunity to calm down and think more clearly about the situation.

Stay Motivated

As the case study illustrates, it is easy for you to become discouraged or the target of a disgruntled provider. Dealing with complaints and problems day after day can be stressful. What can you do to stay motivated?

Confide in Someone

You need to have someone you can talk to daily, especially when you have had a difficult day. You should expect support from your fellow staff or your supervisor. In our case study, Sarah has Jean to help her put her hurt feelings in perspective. Other home visitors are another good source of support. It is always comforting to know that others have faced similar situations.

Meet with Other Home Visitors

Establishing regular home visitor meetings with others in your organization or in your community gives you an opportunity to share common problems and solutions. Usually whenever a group of home visitors gets together in the same room, there is never a lack of topics to discuss. Your enthusiasm, common experiences, and solutions motivate you to try some new tactics in the field.

Acknowledge Success

Reflect on positive changes that you have observed in some of your clients. Take the time to pat yourself on the back and to acknowledge the part you played in creating positive influences on providers, children, and families.

Let Go

You can lead a horse to water, but you can't make it drink. Acknowledge the fact that some things are out of your control. Occasionally you may deal with a provider who does not meet a goal, no matter what you say and do. Becoming frustrated causes discouragement. Set limits on how much time and effort you put into this situation. Recognize when to let go.

Take Good Care of Yourself

You have a very demanding job; you need to get enough rest and to eat a healthy diet. If you are experiencing a problem in your personal life, share it with a trusted friend or colleague. Often just being able to talk relieves some of the stress.

Keep True to Your Values

Remember your values and give yourself credit for honoring them. In the case study, Sarah needs to give herself credit for putting the children's safety first even though it creates an uncomfortable situation.

Set New Goals for Yourself

Nothing is more intrinsically motivating than successfully meeting goals. Set realistic short- and long-term goals.

Celebrate Your Accomplishments

Especially when you are discouraged, you may forget the good things you have done. Keep a success diary and jot down notes when you are especially pleased or proud of yourself. When you become discouraged, read your diary and remind yourself of the positive changes you have helped a provider make, the personal goals you have met, and any problems you have successfully solved.

· · · · · · · ·

You encounter failure in your job. It is natural to become frustrated and disappointed when you feel you have failed. But dwelling on these negative feelings has a definite effect on your own motivation and how you motivate others.

Instead, use unsatisfactory situations as opportunities for evaluation and reflection. Learn and move on. Your job is complex and difficult, and each time you motivate people to make a positive change, you have made a difference in their lives and in the lives of those around them.

 CHECKPOINT—Your Motivation Skills

When you want to inspire intrinsic motivation, use the following checklist to prepare for a visit.

1. Think about what you know about the provider.

   ○ Experience

   ○ Personality or communication style

2. Identify the exact long-term goal you want to motivate the provider to attain.

3. Break the long-term goal into small, attainable goals.

4. Determine the importance of the goals and when you should present the information to the provider:

   ○ Individually, while the children are awake

   ○ Individually, during naptime

   ○ Collectively, at a group meeting in the evening or on a Saturday

5. Gather facts and other information to help the provider see the value in attaining these goals.

6. Develop specific instruction that explains what you expect from the providers.

7. Develop a time frame for her to implement the goals.

8. Determine how you are going to provide helpful feedback to her.

9. Think and be positive!

Module 8

Understand How Adults Learn

Module Description

An essential part of a home visitor's job is training and imparting knowledge to providers. The child care providers you visit obtain training for many different reasons, from being mandated to obtain a set number of hours of training per year to attending trainings to improve skills. The training you do can range from educating providers about serious regulatory issues to giving them knowledge of fun, age-appropriate activities for the children. Whether a training session is serious, informative, or mandatory, you need to ensure it is meaningful. Making it so begins by understanding how adults learn. Only when you have this knowledge can you devise training opportunities that are effective for your clients.

This module will help you provide the best trainings by applying proper methodologies. It is based on research and provides factual information and useful strategies.

Learning Objectives

- Understand the barriers that hinder adults from learning new skills.
- Be able to partner with adults in learning and teaching new skills.
- Know how to give proper positive and negative feedback to adults.
- Recognize how important your body language is when teaching adults.
- Be familiar with adult learning styles.
- Respect how culture and beliefs can influence learning.

. . . .

Case Study
. . . .

Ben is the home visitor responsible for thirty providers in his organization. Ben's state child care licensing agency is requiring that all child care providers adopt the newest information on sudden infant death syndrome (SIDS) safe sleeping requirements. Ben has been assigned to teach the providers these requirements. He is planning a two-hour workshop for his providers to be followed by additional training when he conducts home visits. In planning his workshop, Ben considers what he knows about successfully training adults.

First, Ben identifies the barriers that could hinder some of his providers from attending the training or receiving its full benefits. He knows his providers have very busy schedules. They work all day and have family responsibilities at night. He acknowledges that his providers are often exhausted in the evenings and find it hard to concentrate. He realizes he must schedule the training at a convenient time when the providers can concentrate on his topic. He decides to hold the training early on a Saturday morning.

Next Ben thinks about his providers' typical level of experience. He knows the majority have been operating their child care businesses for longer than five years. Therefore, he knows he must incorporate their experience into the training and praise them for their hard work.

Ben also acknowledges that many of his providers are used to doing things a certain way and may not appreciate being told to make changes. He must make a connection between what the providers are already doing and the new skills he will introduce. Ben knows providers must see the relevance and value of the new procedure to be motivated to adopt it. He decides to present this information as a problem all providers face and guide them toward the solution.

Ben is also aware that as a male home visitor of large stature, he needs to be careful not to intimidate his clients. Because he often finds it difficult to adopt the role of a facilitator partnering with a provider, he knows he will have to work very hard not to act like an authoritative lecturer.

Ben also knows he must address different learning styles in his presentation. He plans to use handouts, small discussion groups that allow providers the opportunity to share their thoughts and feelings, and role-playing opportunities. He wants to minimize lecturing because he knows the providers will respond more positively to being guided toward individual goals.

After thinking through these important points, Ben is ready to plan the content of his workshop. He is confident that by reexamining the important points on how his providers learn, he can present a meaningful workshop.

. . . .

Adult Learning

Pedagogy describes the art and practice of teaching in formal education, usually to children. In his book *The Modern Practice of Adult Education: Andragogy versus Pedagogy* (1970), Malcolm S. Knowles introduces the term *andragogy* in discussing adult learning to North American teachers. Teachers of children know it is unnecessary to refer to a child's experience when introducing a new concept, because newness is commonplace to young children. Knowles maintains that adults learn differently because they understand and retain information best when they can relate it to their prior and present experience.

Behind the term *andragogy* are the following assumptions:

- Adults can self-direct their own learning.
- Adults need to know why they need the knowledge.
- Adults have years of experience that influence new learning; as a result, they favor experiential learning, which means learning by direct experience.
- Adults want to learn and immediately use the knowledge.

Relating information to the adult learner's experiences facilitates learning. Therefore, before training adults, you should have an understanding of the educational and experience levels of the learners. For example, when you are training licensed family child care providers, you know that they have an understanding of the regulations that govern their operations. You should also take into consideration the number of years the providers have been giving care. Asking questions and closely observing will give you a basis to build the new learning on. It is also necessary to pay attention to how you present the content of your training. Acknowledging and respecting the experience the providers have opens the way for acceptance of the new skills, concepts, or behavior being taught. What does effective teaching begin with? The answer is respect.

Make It Relevant and Personal

For adult learners, certain key principles need to be addressed as part of any training. Since family child care providers work long hours and have very busy schedules, they need to know the objectives of the training and how it applies to their own lives. They also need to know why they must learn the material and under what circumstances they will be expected to demonstrate their learning. Providers learn the new concepts more readily when they can apply learning to what they already know. Adopting these principles will make your trainings relevant and personal for the providers.

Unique Barriers to Learning

Child care providers balance family and child care responsibilities. This leaves little time for them to learn new skills. Many providers also come to formal training with "baggage," such as negative school experiences that may undermine their confidence in learning and succeeding. Most of the training you offer takes place in a setting that creates other barriers to learning: the home child care environment. When you visit a provider, the children she cares for often show off or demand extra attention. This makes it even more difficult for the provider to concentrate on what you are trying to teach her.

Anticipating these barriers can help you create more successful visits. For example, always take into consideration the seriousness and complexity of the information you are presenting. Ask yourself if the information can be given to the provider as a handout for her to read later or if the technical information requires you to guide her through it. Depending on the seriousness and complexity of the training materials, you may want to schedule the training during naptime or another time when the provider can give her full attention to the materials. Training on a curriculum activity can occur with the children present. Training on how to complete a required form, on the other hand, demands the provider's complete attention.

When addressing barriers that stem from attitudes and beliefs, you need to help providers rid themselves of false notions. For example, many adults believe that they are too old to learn something new. This is far from the truth. In a recent *MIT News* article, Cathryn Delude reports that neuroscientists at MIT have found that the adult brain can not only adapt to new circumstances but also adapt and change very quickly. The adult brain can make new connections when needed and speedily adapt to new experiences (Delude 2009). The adult brain can grow and make connections to accommodate new information. In fact, adults have an advantage over children because we already have experience and knowledge to connect new information to.

Transfer of Knowledge

The best way to demonstrate the relevancy of new information is to connect it to what a person already knows and does. This immediately suggests to the learner how to apply the new information, giving it value. When training providers, you must help them take what they are learning and transfer it to their own situations. This is termed the *transfer of knowledge,* and it must occur for providers to understand new information. For example, when Ben instructs his providers on safe sleeping requirements, he relates this information to what the providers already know about Sudden Infant Death Syndrome and shows them how to apply it to their naptime routines.

When the transfer of knowledge occurs, you can feel confident that providers will apply what they have learned. Transfer of knowledge involves the learner's attitude toward the information provided to her; from it, she forges something new: knowledge made up of new information and her own experience. To assure the transfer of knowledge, consider these factors:

- Is the information relevant to the providers?
- Does the training assume a level of experience that the provider has reached?
- Do you and your organization place value on the knowledge being taught?
- Do you follow up to see if providers are implementing the goals of the training?
- Will the providers be using their new training skills immediately or in the future?
- Are the goals and expectations you have for the providers clearly stated?

Referring to the case study at the beginning of this module, here's how Ben would answer the questions:

- Is the information relevant to the providers being trained? It is very relevant to the providers, because naptime is part of their daily schedules. In addition, this new procedure is part of the requirements of their licensing, and they must comply.
- Does the training assume a level of experience that the providers have? All of Ben's providers know the regulations and recognize

they must comply to maintain their licenses. All of his providers care for infants in their programs.

- Do you and your organization place value on the information being taught? Ben knows he is introducing a life-saving procedure, so he places a very high value on the information.
- Do you follow up to see if providers are implementing the goals of the training? Because this is a regulatory requirement, Ben will be checking compliance when he makes his monthly visits to the providers. If a provider is not complying, he will review the procedure and inform her of the consequences of not complying.
- Will the providers be using their new training skills immediately or in the future? Ben expects to see the new procedures implemented immediately.
- Are the goals and expectations you have for the providers clearly stated? Ben will ask the providers to sign a statement attesting that they have learned the new procedure and that they understand it must be implemented immediately. A copy of the statement will be given to each provider so she cannot misunderstand the expectations.

As you can see, there are many aspects to consider when preparing for the transfer of knowledge. Discuss the ways they can use the information with providers; doing so will help transfer the knowledge into their daily routines. If you are conducting a group training, provide practice sessions so your clients can see the new skills being used in real-life situations. Allow them the opportunity to discuss any barriers they may have to adopting the new skills.

For example, suppose you are training providers to observe the preschoolers in their care in order to assess them. One provider complains that she does not have time to sit, observe, and document a preschooler's activity because she has other toddlers and an infant whom she needs to supervise. Recognizing this as a very real barrier to transferring knowledge into practice, you should address it before the provider attempts to apply the skill. If you are conducting a group training, you can have providers brainstorm on how to overcome this barrier. If you are conducting a one-on-one training in the provider's home, you can brainstorm one-to-one with the provider on ways to overcome the barrier. You may even want to demonstrate a suggested solution.

Transfer of knowledge is an essential part of adult learning. Use the above suggestions, ask yourself the questions, and follow up to ensure that the training skills are being put into practice.

Relating to What Is Known

Home visitors are often asked to teach providers new policies, procedures, updated information, best practices, and even technology. When your teaching is effective, your clients change their behavior, gain skills and knowledge, and even improve their attitude.

Many of the providers you visit have had years of experience. Be aware of this. Because adults evaluate new information by what they already know, if you are teaching them something that goes against what they already know, they are likely to reject it. Often you hear "I've always done it this way" or "I tried that and it doesn't work."

In terms of receptiveness to new ideas, providers fall into different categories, depending on where they are in their child care careers. Look at each provider individually to determine where she stands:

- A provider may be relatively new; she does not have a lot of experience to relate to the new training. You need to connect her to the new knowledge by making sure that she understands any key words or practices related to the training goals.
- A provider may be new but have an early childhood degree. The early childhood degree gives her knowledge of child development, but she may lack experience in applying it on a daily basis.
- A provider may have a combination of a formal early childhood education and years of experience caring for children. She may be very set in her ways, so it is essential that she understand the relevance of the new learning to what she is already doing. She may be a wonderful resource to help new, inexperienced providers meet training goals.
- A provider may have been caring for children for many years and be set in her ways, based on experience rather than formal education in child development. She may need to be convinced that the new goals are relevant to her everyday schedule. Her long experience can help her to implement the new goals. However, her lack of

child developmental knowledge may hinder her in understanding the reasons for the new goals.

Below are some strategies that apply to all categories:

- Give the provider a chance to express how she feels about the new training or requirement.
- Acknowledge her experience and mention positive skills or behaviors you have observed her using. This can give her confidence to learn a new skill or concept.
- Ask questions throughout the training and encourage the provider to express how she see herself using the information you present.

Treating Adults Like Adults

A home visitor should never talk down to a provider. Listen carefully to her comments, objections, or suggestions. Always be respectful of her point of view. At times this can be difficult; perhaps you are instructing a provider on how to comply with a regulation or you have to address a serious health or safety issue. When you listen respectfully and ask questions, you show the provider your willingness to work together, even in the toughest situations. Whenever you present information, remember to ask the provider if she has any experiences that could apply to the new information. Providers nearly always have something important to add to a discussion.

Overcoming Fear of Mistakes

Adults are more conscious than children of making mistakes. Children love to show off their accomplishments. When you walk into a room of them, you often hear, "Look at me!" "See what I can do?" "Look at my picture! Isn't it great?" Over time, this freedom of expression becomes lost and a fear of making mistakes develops. Some of your clients may have low self-esteem and feel they cannot learn something new. Being sensitive to this fear of failure or of looking foolish is very important when you are teaching adults. Never judge the provider, and do not feed into her negativity. Using praise and pointing out the valuable things she is doing helps you instill confidence in her to try new things. Helping her take small steps encourages her to experience small successes—all leading to the larger goal.

Learning through Problem Solving

The knowledge that you share with a provider should offer positive, concrete solutions to real-life problems. For example, suppose a provider is having a problem incorporating age-appropriate activities into her schedule. You are in the position to train her about the activities that are appropriate for the children in her care. Presenting the information as a solution to the problem and helping the provider decide how to incorporate the information into her schedule will assist her in transferring the knowledge into positive actions.

Presenting new information by starting with a problem that many other providers face emphasizes the relevance to an individual provider. Occasionally a provider may insist that her problem is entirely different. She may agree with what you are saying, but she has reasons why it would not work for her. Give that provider the chance to explain why her problem is unique, then identify how the solution you've presented can be used in many situations, including her unique one.

For example, in the case study, Ben recognizes that all providers caring for babies face the possibility of a child succumbing to sudden infant death syndrome. When Ben offers instruction about preventing SIDS, one provider tells him that she has a baby who absolutely will not sleep on his back. She argues that she has tried, but the baby will only sleep on his stomach. Ben knows the regulation is non-negotiable. Nonetheless, he listens to the provider respectfully and assures her that the baby will adapt and that she must comply.

> *The following are examples of mnemonic devices:*
>
> - *Remembering the number of days in a month—"Thirty days has September, April, June, and November. All the rest have thirty-one except February."*
> - *When assessing an emergency situation, people use ABC— Airway: Is the person's airway clear? Breathing: Is the person breathing? Cardio/Circulation: Is the person's heart beating?*
> - *Singing with children during cleanup and hand-washing time triggers their memory to complete a task.*

Individual Learning Styles

Adults can adapt to many types of teaching styles; everyone has a preference for how she receives information Each of us has an individual learning style that is most comfortable. To be really effective, you need to get to know your clients' preferences. Adult learners fall into three main categories.

VISUAL LEARNERS

These learners respond well to handouts and written information. Pictures and diagrams of concepts are helpful to them. They learn well from videos. Visual learners are also sensitive to your facial expressions and body language.

AUDITORY LEARNERS

These learners need to hear instructions. Giving clear verbal instructions is essential when teaching them. They also enjoy small group discussions, because these allow them to talk and to hear others' points of view. Verbal cues and mnemonic devices help auditory learners remember the information. Mnemonic devices help stimulate the memory to remember important information; they can be rhymes, songs, or letters of the alphabet.

KINESTHETIC LEARNERS

These people learn by doing. When training kinesthetic learners, you must allow them to practice the new skill. In group training, role playing and practice sessions are helpful.

. . . .

In summary, when you conduct group training, make sure you use a variety of training methods and information so you can reach each type of learner. When you conduct one-on-one training in a provider's home, know her learning style so you can use the most effective one.

Beliefs and Values

Providers have very diverse beliefs and values. You should be respectful and sensitive to issues that may arise from these. For example, a provider's beliefs about authority and control, gender, sense of time, and caring for children may be different from yours.

Reflecting on your own beliefs and values can help you conduct your training respectfully. Here are four things to examine about yourself:

1. Are you as careful with your facial expressions and body language as you are with your words? For example, you may be encouraging the provider with your words, but your body language is saying, "What an odd point of view."
2. Think about whether or not certain personal characteristics or approaches to child care make you uncomfortable.
3. Think about how you feel when talking to people who do not speak English well. Do you avoid speaking to them?
4. Think about any preconceived expectations, or lack of expectations, you have about a particular ethnic or cultural group.

Whether you are training providers in their homes or in groups, knowing how adults learn will be useful. The more you can assist providers to use what they learn, the easier it will be for them to remember the information and apply it in a positive way.

Be a Facilitator

What does it mean to be a facilitator? *Facilitate* means to assist or aid. As a home visitor, you are a facilitator because you assist a provider in her learning. That learning is a collaborative effort. She learns best when you allow her to control what she learns and to decide on her own goals.

Most providers do not like to be told what to do and how to do it. Therefore, avoid the lecture style of teaching as much as possible. Think about how you would react to being told what to do and how to do it. For example, imagine that your supervisor wants you to change the way you schedule your visits. She wants you to conduct them in alphabetical order instead of in order of location. You want to explain that it will take you twice as long to do your job because you will be traveling back and forth between areas, crossing your own path numerous times a day. However, your supervisor simply tells you to do it that way. She provides no reasons for why it is necessary, nor does she give you a chance to talk about it.

Think about how you would feel. Would you be resentful, frustrated, even angry? Take the time to put yourself in your providers' shoes. They are used to carrying out their schedule and responsibilities in their own ways. If you simply tell them they have to do things differently, giving them no reasons, they are likely to become frustrated, resentful, and angry. Remember—adults need to see the reasons and importance of applying training concepts.

Once you embrace your role as a facilitator, you can spend time assisting providers to identify the information important to them. After you know what a provider deems important, you can partner with her to come up with new goals and the steps necessary to reach those goals.

As a facilitator, you create an atmosphere of respect and trust. That atmosphere encourages providers to be more open with you. Brainstorming is an excellent way to encourage providers to express their ideas. Whether you are working with a group or an individual, brainstorming stimulates conversations with providers in which they can express their views and talk about their experiences in relation to the training. Identifying problems together and collaboratively discussing solutions are excellent ways to guide every provider to the solution that is best for her. Allowing the provider the freedom to reflect on what she knows and believes supports her self-direction and ownership of her learning.

Be a Motivator

Ben's SIDS training is mandatory and part of his providers' licensing requirements. But Ben wants his providers to be motivated to adopt the new procedures into their daily routine because they understand and agree with the new policy—not just because it's required.

In module 7, we discussed motivational skills, but it is important to note in the context of the present module that adult learners need more than self-motivation in order to learn. Learning simply for the sake of learning does not usually motivate adults. You cannot motivate providers by giving them stickers or stars, as you can children; instead, they must understand why the outcome of the learning will be practical and beneficial for them. Learning how to use the knowledge is important, but for adults, the motivator is the reward.

Intrinsic motivators come from within. Feelings of self-achievement and satisfaction at meeting a goal can motivate a person. Extrinsic motivators are external; for example, a provider may be motivated if she thinks she may receive a tangible reward or avoid an unpleasant consequence.

Intrinsic rewards are very important to adults. To remain motivated, adults need to feel that learning, acting on the learning, and adopting it as part of their belief system will benefit themselves or others. In the case study, Ben is training his clients about a regulatory requirement. He explains that they must adopt the Safe Sleeping Procedure. Knowing that adults learn and adopt new learning better when they see how it relates to their own situations, Ben has shown them the basis for adopting this policy. He has also praised and recognized their commitment to keeping the infants in their care safe. His praise and commendation give the providers an intrinsic reward by instilling in them a sense of achievement and accomplishment: they are being reminded that they are keeping infants safe.

Preparing Providers for Learning

Prepare providers for learning by letting them know you will assist them throughout the learning process. To motivate your clients, be enthusiastic about the training. While presenting the information, break it down into small objectives and goals. Make sure the providers have a thorough understanding of what they need to do. These steps to success build upon each other, giving providers the motivation to continue on to the next goal.

Meeting Clients' Expectations

Your clients bring their own expectations and needs to your trainings. You must set realistic expectations for each training you provide. To do this, you must know what your clients expect from the training. An excellent way to learn this is to ask the providers at the beginning of the training why they have attended and what they expect to be able to do at the completion of the training. Write these expectations down on a white board or large piece of paper attached to the wall. During the training, refer to the list of expectations to make sure you are meeting your clients' needs, and explain why you may not be addressing some of the expectations during this particular training. At the conclusion, go over each expectation that was met and solicit questions. When you have met the expectations of the providers, you can feel confident that your training was successful.

Give Feedback

Feedback is a very important aspect of adult learning. Your feedback allows providers to evaluate how well they are progressing toward a goal. It also helps providers understand how well they are mastering new skills. Finally, your feedback helps them stay motivated to reach new goals. As beneficial as your feedback is, providers are also encouraged by the feedback they receive from the children when they institute a new practice or activity. After a training, we are always eager to see evaluations from the participants. We read every one, and we particularly appreciate those that offer specific feedback. Feedback that simply says "good" or "good job" does not give me the kind of valuable information I receive from statements like "I particularly enjoyed information on _____ because _____" or "I found the handout on _____ informative."

Similarly, you need to give specific feedback to providers. Be sure to acknowledge their effort to adopt the new learning. Your feedback should be unique for each provider, since each one has different opportunities for acting on the information.

For example, you could say by way of acknowledgment, "Your fixed-up quiet reading corner for the preschoolers looks very inviting. I love the books you have chosen, and the comfortable pillows in the corner look like a cozy place to read a book." Then you can help the provider to the next level: "Do you think you could add story time into your schedule every day, and read the children some of the books to encourage them to become familiar with the stories?" This feedback specifically tells the provider what she has done right, presents the next goal, and specifically states what she needs to do to reach that goal.

Occasionally you may have to give negative feedback. When it is necessary for you to correct a provider, always offer positive feedback first. It is often a good idea to give positive feedback, then corrective feedback, and finally some more positive feedback. Ending with a positive statement encourages the provider. For example, "We talked about the importance of having books available to the preschoolers. I noticed you purchased a wonderful low bookshelf, but it has been a month and there are no books in it. Do you think you might add some books before my next visit?" Then add, "I can give you a wonderful list of books for the children if you need it. The children are going to love this reading area!"

Feedback that is relevant reinforces learning. It also assists providers in redirecting their actions when they are not meeting their goals.

 CHECKPOINT—Thinking about Training Adults

Answer the following questions when you are preparing to train providers, whether in an individual's home or a group.

- Whom are you training?
- What do you know about the learners?
- Why do your clients need this training?
- How will they benefit from the training?
- How can you make the training relevant to their current practices?
- Are there any beliefs or values you should be aware of?
- Are there specific barriers to learning that you should address before the training?
- How will you address audio, visual, and kinesthetic learners?

- What are the goals and objectives of this training?

- How can you break down the goals into small steps?

- How will you provide feedback (verbal, written, follow-up visit, etc.)?

- What type of instrument will you provide so providers can evaluate your performance?

Module 9

Take Ethical Actions

Module Description

. . . .

The situations home visitors face are as varied as the personalities of the individuals they visit. You must balance your responsibilities to a number of parties:

- Society in general—You are in a position to be a role model.
- Your organization—You are hired to ensure that contractual and regulatory policies are carried out.
- The individuals you visit—You are in a position of leadership, and providers look to you for guidance.
- The families of the children you observe—Your observations assist in maintaining a safe and healthy environment for the children.
- Yourself—You need to know you are doing the right thing.

Balancing these responsibilities often creates gray areas—decision-making points with no clearly right or wrong solution. For example, you may need to choose between the trust the provider has put in you and loyalty to your organization.

This module discusses the importance of developing a professional code of ethics. A code of ethics helps you set standards and guidelines for solving ethical dilemmas before they arise. If you are working without a code of ethics, you may be crossing boundaries that can seriously hinder your ability to conduct objective observations.

Learning Objectives

- Understand your role as a professional.
- Establish clear professional boundaries with your clients.
- Know and follow professional boundaries with regard to money.

· · · · · · · · ·

Case Study

Mei has been visiting Sonja for a few years. She has always found Sonja reliable and responsible. On Mei's current visit, she finds Sonja crying. Sonja tells Mei that her car is going to be repossessed if she cannot make the payment today. Sonja looks at Mei with tears in her eyes and asks Mei if she can loan her the money for the payment. She promises to repay Mei as soon as her check comes in at the end of the month. Sonja points out that she needs her car to successfully operate her child care business. Without a car, she will find it difficult to get groceries and pick up or drop off children at their school or home. Sonja tells Mei she may have to close her child care.

Mei does not make a quick decision based on emotion. She takes a few minutes to assess the dilemma. Mei knows that when a child care home closes, she will have to find new placements for the children. Mei realizes that this may be difficult because there are not many openings in the neighborhood. But Mei has been trained not to take ownership of a provider's problem. She recognizes that Sonja's dilemma is not her problem to solve. Any repercussions from Sonja's dilemma may become her problem, but this should not influence her decision.

Mei's thoughts about the dilemma are outlined below. Mei may instinctively want to loan Sonja the money, but she has adopted a code of ethics that demands she go beyond her initial feelings and carefully examine her core principles to see if any ethical standards are involved.

- Reasons to loan the money: Mei feels sorry for Sonja, and it would make her feel good to loan Sonja the money. Doing so would also prevent any problems she would have to solve if Sonja closes her facility.
- Reasons not to loan the money: The first ethical principle that comes to Mei's mind is being responsible. Mei asks herself if her responsibility to her organization conflicts with her responsibility to

the provider. She acknowledges that her first loyalty must be to her organization. Mei's employer expects her to remain objective and to accurately assess the services Sonja provides. In examining these responsibilities, Mei finds she would be jeopardizing her ability to be objective; she also realizes that addressing Sonja's financial situation is not one of her job duties.

Mei's organization has a code of ethics that discusses the principle of accepting money from a client. The same information applies if the client were to accept money from Mei. That action would change the relationship between Mei and her client. Mei is not trained to provide financial information. By loaning Sonja money, she could be setting herself up to take on the responsibility of advising her client about her financial situation. This could result in serious ramifications. For example, if Mei's advice failed, Sonja would then have reason to blame Mei for the failure. Mei realizes that Sonja would have reason to transfer the problem to her, perhaps viewing it now as Mei's problem to solve if she wants to be repaid.

Mei has also been trained to ask herself four important questions when she encounters an ethical dilemma:

1. How would others, such as other clients and coworkers, view your ability to remain objective with this provider? Mei knows that the child care providers she services are a close group. She knows that word spreads quickly among them and that what she does for one client may be expected by others. Therefore, should she give Sonja the money, other clients might feel they could ask her for loans. Mei also considers her coworkers. They might not agree with a decision to loan money, fearing that their own clients would begin to ask them for loans.

2. Are you meeting your needs or the needs of the client? Mei now examines her motives for wanting to help Sonja. She admits to herself that she needs to be liked. She also often feels that she must solve everyone's problems. Knowing these things about herself, she looks beyond any immediate satisfaction she might get from loaning Sonja the money. She realizes that she might be only temporarily meeting Sonja's financial needs. Mei acknowledges that she is not addressing the reasons why Sonja is falling behind in her payments, an area that is beyond her expertise.

3. Who will be affected by your actions? After serious reflection, Mei thinks about how other clients could come to view the loan to Sonja as favoritism. She then thinks about her coworkers and how they might find themselves having to defend her actions to their own clients. Mei also realizes that her own family could be affected if Sonja fails to pay back the loan on time. Last, she thinks about how she might be personally affected if she loses her objectivity.

4. What are the short- and long-term effects of your actions? Even though Mei might feel good about helping Sonja, doing so might only put a bandage on a deeper problem. Mei is not in a position to determine the root of the problem, which could be poor money management or living beyond one's means. If Mei were to loan Sonja the money, she would put herself in the uncomfortable position of having to collect the debt. Mei knows she does not want to help Sonja with her personal financial budgeting, which is beyond the scope of Mei's professional relationship or expertise.

    In addition, Mei does not want to put herself in a situation in which she might compromise her ability to be objective. She wonders if she would be putting herself in a conflicting situation by not wanting to report any discrepancies or misconduct on Sonja's part if doing so might result in Sonja's loss of income. Mei might be tempted to compromise her integrity until Sonja repaid the loan.

After careful consideration, Mei realizes that loaning Sonja the money would not be an appropriate ethical decision. She tells Sonja she is very sorry, but her organization's code of ethics does not allow her to make a personal loan to a provider. Mei is very happy she has adopted a code of ethics that helps her examine issues when they arise. She knows she has made the right decision.

· · · · · · · ·

The Importance of Ethics

There are many definitions of ethics. Taken literally, the word *ethics* comes from the Greek word *ethos,* which means character. Aristotle used words that translate to *moral, religious,* and *legal concept* when he spoke of ethics. A common view suggests that ethics are a guideline on how to treat others, based on how you yourself prefer to be treated. Living by ethics means deciding the best course of action for the good of an individual or for a society based on principles, standards, and values.

Many professions adopt a code of ethics as a framework for the values and principles guiding their work. As a home visitor, you face ethical issues every day. You need ethical guidelines to provide professional standards in this field. You are in a position to set professional ethical standards that meet the responsibilities for a variety of people.

- Yourself—You have a duty to yourself to know that you are doing the right thing.
- Your organization—Your employer trusts you to represent the organization.
- Your clients—These include family child care providers, parents, children, and contracting organizations.
- Society in general—Society puts its trusts in a system that monitors and regulates the safety of children.

Everyone has a set of values that govern their decisions. Your family, culture, and experiences largely formulate your values. Examining what your ethical beliefs are and pondering the dilemmas you might face should help you be prepared when challenges arise. Purposefully considering ethics helps you recognize situations in which they should play a role. When you face ethical dilemmas, you can use some of the core principles you have adopted to decide on the best course of action.

Adopt a Code of Ethics

Your organization should have a code of ethics. If you have not seen one, ask your supervisor for a copy. You should examine it in relation to your own values and beliefs. If your organization does not have a written code of ethics, suggest that creating one should become a priority. A code of ethics cannot resolve all problems, but as Mei's case study shows, her organization's code of ethics could be used as a guideline for best practices. Using the code helped her to carry out her professional duties in a fair and respectful way.

Arrange a meeting with other home visitors in your area if your organization does not have a code of ethics. Discuss some of the dilemmas you face, and produce ethical guidelines that would address them. A code of ethics is a valuable tool that gives you the ideals and the language to express your profession's values. Creating a code of ethics encourages you to examine your personal values, beliefs, strengths, conflicts, and limitations, and to see if they are similar to those of others in your profession. You may find your views and beliefs challenged when you listen to others. In defending your own viewpoint, you can clarify what ethical action to take. (Of course, if you are discussing specific cases with your peers, you must remember to maintain confidentiality.)

When dealing with ethical issues, you often find that there is no right or wrong answer. Nonetheless, following a professional code of ethics for home visitors gives you a measure of assurance that you are behaving in ways that are in the best interest of your clients. A code of ethics protects providers from abuse by assuring that you are performing your job as directed by moral standards accepted by other home visiting professionals.

A code of ethics should address the following core principles:

Trust

This standard of behavior includes always keeping your word. When you are consistently reliable, you create trust between you and the individuals with whom you work.

Respect

You demonstrate respect for others' beliefs, whether those are based on religion, personal morals, ethnicity, or culture. You never impose your religious, moral, or political beliefs on a client.

Conflicts may arise between a client's beliefs and your organization's requirements. You need to be able to resolve the problem while still showing respect for her beliefs. You must balance the client's beliefs with the changes you need her to make to comply with your organization's regulations.

Confidentiality

Be respectful of clients' rights to privacy. Especially because you are dealing with children and their families, you must protect everyone in your program. Adopt the following policies:

- Never leave notes, paperwork, or documentation about a client's or family's private information where it can be read by others.
- Never discuss a client's personal information or any information about the children she is caring for in a public setting. You never know who may overhear your conversation.
- Be aware that when personal information is left on answering machines or sent by e-mail, anyone who has access to these messages

can listen to or read them. Take immediate action to delete or move information to a protected file.

- You should never try to get a client to divulge personal information that is not necessary or is not related to the services she performs. If she does confide personal information, make every attempt to keep it confidential.

Responsibility

You should be responsible for doing what is best for the clients you visit. However, you might find yourself in the uncomfortable position of being responsible to conflicting parties. You might have legal, contractual, or employment obligations that must be met and that supersede your responsibility to the client. For example, the law mandates that you report suspected child abuse or neglect, whether you suspect the provider or someone within the child's family. Providers and families should always be informed in advance that you have responsibilities beyond your relationships with them and that you may be mandated to file a report that is detrimental to them.

Decisions on when and what types of gifts to accept should be made after examining the circumstances. Ask yourself: "Why is the gift being given? What is the culture or customs of the person giving the gift? Will accepting the gift compromise my ability to be objective?" Look at the policy of your organization to help you decide what is appropriate. Examine your values, and set a policy on where you draw the line. Let your clients know up front what your policy is, and stick to it. Do not make exceptions. Remember—anytime you accept a gift, you may be compromising your ability to carry out your job duties effectively.

Power

Because you assess the services and behavior of the provider, do not sell products or service to her. She might feel that if she does not buy your product, she will get a bad review. This can lead clients to feel compelled to purchase whatever you are selling, even if you are selling them for someone else.

Accepting Gifts

You should never accept money or expensive gifts from a client. Doing so severely compromises your ability to do your job objectively. Some home visitors feel that homemade gifts or gifts of food are acceptable. In some regions of the United States and among some ethnic groups, not to accept such personal gifts could be considered insulting.

Your Limits

Because you are in a supervisory position and trusted by clients, you may find that they turn to you for advice on other matters. If you are not trained or certified in these areas, do not attempt to give counsel or advice. The following are examples of areas in which you would not want to give counsel:

- Legal: If a provider is having custody issues with her husband and asks for your advice, do not give it.
- Financial: If a provider asks you to recommend investment options, decline.
- Medical: If a provider seeks advice about over-the-counter medication or treatments, recommend she see a doctor.

In many communities, you are likely to come into contact with your clients during non-work-related activities. For example, your families may attend the same religious gatherings, or you may have children who attend the same school, play on the same sports teams, or go to the same dance classes. These contacts should be confined to the context of these activities. Work and work-related issues should not be discussed. Keep in mind that being friendly and becoming a client's friend are two different things.

Conflict of Interest

When you are trying to serve two parties that have a relationship with each other, you need to make your own position very clear to both parties. For example, suppose your own child attends a family child care program that your agency oversees. The agency is awarded a grant for an innovative and award-winning music program to be given to an exemplary provider who has devoted many years to child care. You are asked to recommend the provider who will receive this grant. The first person who comes to mind is a provider who has been caring for children for many years and runs a beautiful, active, caring program. She is also the provider you originally wanted to send your own child to, but the provider did not have an opening then. If you were to reward the provider now, doing so might benefit your own child. Three things need to happen here:

1. Your agency needs to know that your child attends a program the agency oversees.
2. The provider who cares for your child needs to know that you will not play favorites.
3. You should never make an official agency visit to your child's caregiver.

Professional Boundaries

You weaken your position when you do not remain professional and set clear boundaries. This does not mean you shouldn't be sensitive to clients' feelings. Your job is to guide clients in the right direction. You should attempt to empower them to make necessary changes. You should never take on the responsibility of being the solution to their problems.

Think through Ethical Dilemmas

Even with a well-thought-out code of ethics, you may encounter ethical dilemmas or situations in which there is no clear right or wrong answer. Ethical dilemmas often require that you choose between two or more ethical principles, such as trust or loyalty. Doing so can be challenging and stressful. To prepare yourself for such dilemmas, seriously scrutinize how you have handled situations in the past and examine what types of dilemmas you may face in the future.

When you are thinking through ethical dilemmas, consider the effects your decisions may have beyond the immediate situation. Like Mei, you should examine each dilemma by asking yourself these four essential questions:

1. How do others, such as other clients and coworkers, view your ability to remain objective about this client?
2. Are you meeting your needs or the needs of the client?
3. Who will be affected by your actions?
4. What are the short- and long-term effects of your actions?

Using the core principles to develop a code of ethics and asking yourself these questions should help you make sound decisions. Your goal is to avoid any lasting adverse effects on doing your work.

Use the following sample dilemmas to explore your own personal reactions or as topics for discussions between you and other home visitors. Identify any conflicts in the scenarios similar to ones you may have previously encountered, and use the core principles and questions presented in this module to formulate your response.

Scenario

Use the dilemma presented in the case study, but turn it around. You are in danger of having your car repossessed, and a client offers to lend you money to make the payment.

DILEMMA

Accepting money from a client puts you in the position of owing her a favor. This might compromise your ability to be objective during your home visit evaluations.

ASK YOURSELF

- Would you be able to objectively review this client if you owed her money?
- If other clients hear about the loan, might they believe that you will favor the client who gave you the loan?
- How does your organization view taking a loan from a client?
- Even after the loan is repaid, will you feel indebted to the client?
- Examine why you are behind on your car payment. Will the loan solve the problem, or will you be in the same situation next month?

Scenario

You have been visiting a client monthly for a few years. She has always been a very professional and responsible provider. She has a well-thought-out schedule that incorporates age-appropriate activities for the children. During your last few visits, you have noticed that the provider appears to have lost weight and has dark circles under her eyes. During your current visit, she confides in you that her husband has left her and she has taken a second job at night to pay the mortgage. Even so, she is afraid she will lose her house. She also assures you that she is not too tired to take care of the six preschoolers in her care.

DILEMMA

Having heard this new information, you are concerned that the provider may not be as diligent as she should be in watching the children. You are concerned that she might even doze off, putting the children in danger. However, you have no evidence that she is not being diligent. You also acknowledge to yourself that if you were to remove the children, you would be putting her in an even worse financial situation.

ASK YOURSELF

- Do you honor the confidentiality of the client?
- Do you break that confidentiality and move the children to another provider?
- Does your state have child care licensing regulations that address additional employment?

- Is the provider in violation of these regulations?
- If a child were injured because the provider was not as alert as she should be, do you, as the home visitor, bear the responsibility?

Scenario

A parent calls you and requests a referral to one of your child care providers. She wants a provider who only cares for Caucasian children—she does not want her child in care with any other race or nationality. Your supervisor is a personal friend of this parent and asks you to try to meet the parent's requirements.

DILEMMA

Your personal belief is that the nationality or color of the children should not be a priority in selecting a child care facility. You do not categorize your clients by the color or the nationality of the families they serve. Your organization has a nondiscriminatory policy.

ASK YOURSELF

- Because your supervisor instructed you to meet the parent's requirements, does that absolve you from going against your personal beliefs and those of your organization?
- If other parents and providers learn that you have discriminated against them in the placement of this child, what could it do to your reputation?
- How might your decision affect the respect and trust your clients have in you?

Scenario

You are assigned a new client to supervise and visit. The new client is your best friend.

DILEMMA

The client has been your friend for many years, and you have always helped and supported each other. You know that even though she says she does not expect special treatment, she is expecting that you will look out for her best interest.

ASK YOURSELF

- Can you supervise your best friend objectively?
- Should you disclose to your supervisor that the new client is your best friend?

Scenario

You have a waiting list of parents who are looking for child care in your clients' homes. You get a call from your director, who informs you that her niece needs child care immediately. She asks you to please put her niece at the top of the waiting list.

DILEMMA

Each month, when you update your waiting list, you let parents know where they are on the list. You personally assure the parents that their children will be offered care in the order of their position on the list. Because the parents on the list trust you, how should you handle this request?

ASK YOURSELF

- What is your responsibility to the parents on your waiting list?
- What is your responsibility to your director? Should you place her niece at the top of the list?
- What could happen to your reputation if you put your director's niece on the top of the list and other parents found out about it?
- How might your director react if you refuse to put her niece on top of the list?

 CHECKPOINT—Ethics

We hope you have found the information in this chapter on ethics thought provoking and informative. Use the following checklist to help you make decisions presented by ethical dilemmas.

1. In making your decision, might any of the following be affected by your decision?

   ○ Other clients   YES | NO

   ○ Coworkers   YES | NO

   ○ Families or children serviced   YES | NO

   ○ Your ability to remain objective   YES | NO

2. Are you focused on meeting your needs?   YES | NO

   ○ Are you focused on meeting the needs of the client?   YES | NO

3. Will any of the following be affected by your actions?

   ◦ Your employer   YES | NO

   ◦ Colleagues   YES | NO

   ◦ State or federal contracting agencies   YES | NO

   ◦ Other clients you service   YES | NO

   ◦ Families or children in care   YES | NO

4. Will any short-term effects result from your decision?   YES | NO

   ◦ If yes, name the effects.

5. Will any long-term effects result from your decision?   YES | NO

   ◦ If yes, name the effects.

Module 10

Consider Legalities

Module Description

When interacting with providers and families, home visitors must be aware of the city and state regulations that providers must adhere to. These regulations include licensing requirements, which are particularly important for you to know.

Knowledge of all regulations applying to your clients will help you address problems before they become issues. You can't just know *about* them, though. You need to have a thorough understanding of all the regulations affecting your clients.

Besides regulations, many laws pertain to child care, such as those addressing custody, child safety, and neglect. You will find that some states interpret the laws differently. Many times providers will ask for your guidance when they are faced with a legal issue. Although you should not put yourself in the position of giving legal advice, you should know where they can find the pertinent laws addressing their situations. Knowing about the laws and being able to guide your clients to what the laws are and where they can be found will protect you and your clients from possible legal action. You should always be aware of situations that may become legal problems. This module will give you information in all of these areas. If you have any questions about the legality of a course of conduct, you should discuss it with members of your organization and/or a lawyer.

Learning Objectives

- Understand the importance of child care licensing regulations.
- Be aware of the types of situations resulting from entering and being in private homes that could result in a lawsuit.
- Understand the importance of laws and regulations that affect your work and the work of family child care providers.

. . . .

Case Study

Tanya is a new home visitor who has been on the job for less than a year. She has an outgoing and friendly manner, and the clients she serves have quickly become comfortable with her and welcome her visits.

Today Tanya is visiting Lila. Lila has been caring for income-eligible children for quite a few years and is always meticulous in her paperwork and documentation of attendance. Lila is very committed to the program and even accepts a lower rate for income eligible children than her private rate. Lila is a kind and giving person who dislikes any confrontation.

When Tanya first arrives today at Lila's child care, Lila is waiting for her and welcomes her in. Tanya soon realizes that Lila seems a little distracted. Tanya asks her if anything is bothering her. Lila says, "Yes, I have something you should know, but I don't want the parent to know that it came from me. If I tell you, you cannot tell anyone that I am the one who told you."

Tanya received home visiting training before she started her job. One of the points emphasized in her training was never to agree to confidentiality until she knows what she is agreeing to. She cannot agree to keep a secret if doing so conflicts with any of the legal or regulatory requirements that are responsibilities of her job. Before Lila continues, Tanya tells her she cannot promise confidentiality until she hears what Lila has to say. Lila thinks for a minute and decides to tell Tanya what is on her mind.

Lila tells Tanya that the mother of one of the children she cares for is committing fraud. The child's father has moved back into the home, and the mother is not notifying the welfare agency that pays for her child care, because she does not want to lose her subsidy. When Tanya hears this information, she is very glad that she did not promise Lila confidentiality.

Tanya now finds herself in a position of having knowledge of possible welfare fraud in her program. She has an ethical and legal responsibility to document this discussion and to disclose this information to her immediate supervisor. Tanya thanks Lila for her honesty and commends her for doing the right thing. Even though Lila is still apprehensive about the parent learning that the information has come from her, Tanya reassures her that she made a wise decision by reporting this.

Tanya documents her conversation with Lila. She brings the documentation to her supervisor to initiate an investigation. Tanya gets annoyed when she hears of families that take advantage of the child care subsidies, because she knows that many deserving parents are waiting for subsidized child care slots to become available. She hopes that if the accusations are correct, she will be helping a truly deserving family.

• • • • • • • • •

Understand the Law

Often clients turn to home visitors when they are faced with legal problems arising from their child care business or the families they service. Although you are not a lawyer and we do *not* advocate your giving legal advice, you must learn the laws and regulations affecting you and your clients. You are certainly in a position to advocate for and assist clients when they encounter legal or regulatory issues. Being familiar with the laws and regulations helps you guide your clients so they can find answers. You can also discuss possible solutions with them.

You will often find a relationship between legal and ethical issues. However, not all legal issues are ethical and not all ethical issues are legal. Something else to keep in mind is that states may interpret laws differently.

You do not want to give out legal advice if you are not sure of the information. Never give information from undocumented secondhand sources—for example, "I know someone who . . ." Becoming aware of the legal problems your clients might face and guiding them to regulations, specific laws, and documentation they should have in their files help you to protect them from serious lawsuits. Some laws are important for you to be aware of to protect yourself and your clients from legal problems.

Mandated Reporting

Each state has laws about reporting child abuse and/or neglect. You must familiarize yourself with your state's laws, because as a home visitor, you are mandated to report any suspected abuse or neglect.

Each state is responsible for adopting statutes that define abuse and neglect. Know where to find the statutes and be clear about what they say. Contact your local child protective agency for the specific laws, definitions, and procedures for filing. Another excellent resource for mandatory reporters is the Child Welfare Information Gateway Web site, which can connect you with the specific laws in your state: www.childwelfare.gov/systemwide/laws_policies/statutes/manda.pdf.

In most states, if a mandated reporter knowingly fails to report, that person may be guilty of a gross misdemeanor and face jail or fines. Mandated reporters are protected by the law and cannot be sued for making reports that are not substantiated. You do, however, have to have a reasonable suspicion that abuse has occurred.

Often it is the child's provider who brings the information of suspected abuse to your attention. Providers are also mandated reporters; however, they are often apprehensive about reporting because they fear the child will be removed from their care. They may also fear retaliation from the parent or fear that the parent may retaliate against the child. Providers may also be fearful that the child protective agency will not give the parent adequate help or will take the child away. As part of your responsibility to protect the children in the programs you service, you must help providers overcome their fears and report suspected abuse. Carefully go over the documentation of abuse or neglect, encourage the provider, and support her through the process.

If you suspect a provider has abused or neglected the children in her care, you must know your organization's procedures for filing an abuse or neglect claim. Learn what documentation you must provide, whom you need to notify within your organization, and the time frame for filing.

Cell Phone Use

For many home visitors, your car becomes a second office. Because you are on the road so much, your cell phone may be the primary source of communication between you and your clients, your office, and your friends and family. If you answer your phone or make phone calls while on the road, you should be aware of any laws that apply to cell phone use while driving. Statistics have shown that cell phone use while driving is dangerous and the cause of many accidents. Because of this, some states have banned cell phone use by a driver or restricted it to hands-free use. Your organization should set a cell phone use policy, because it can be held liable for your actions while you are working. If your agency has not set a cell phone policy, this does not absolve you from the responsibility of knowing what the law requires and abiding by it.

Giving Out Legal or Medical Information

Occasionally questions may arise concerning the rights of a provider to refuse to release a child to the parent. For example, a provider may ask you what to do when a parent picks up a child without a car seat or when the provider smells alcohol on a parent's breath.

Generally the legal parent or guardian has the right to take the child. However, you can recommend to providers some procedures to help ensure the safety of children. The provider can write a policy into her contract with families that allows her to call another person who is authorized to pick up the child under some circumstances. The circumstances should be clearly listed, such as not releasing the child to a driver who has been drinking. This provision should be clearly explained to the parent or guardian when the contract is signed. If the provider feels that a child is at risk of immediate harm, the provider can call the police. The provider is then in a position to try to stall the parent until the police arrive. Remember that the provider is a mandated reporter and that allowing a child to be driven by an intoxicated adult or without a car seat should be viewed as neglect.

Questions often arise about parents who are going through a divorce. Occasionally one parent instructs the provider not to release the child to the other parent. Again, you do not want to give out legal advice if you are not sure of the information. You should familiarize yourself with terms like *joint custody, joint legal custody, joint physical custody,* and *sole custody.* If you or the provider has never met the noncustodial parent, the provider should request a photograph of that parent for her files. Instructing your clients to clearly understand the custody arrangements for a child and/or any current restraining orders, as well as to keep copies of any legal documents in their files will protect them when problems arise.

Medical Privacy

Most states have laws that prohibit the release of health information without permission. You should know the laws in your state about disclosing personal medical information. Whether or not your state has specific laws regarding medical privacy, including HIV/AIDS, you should advise clients that it is always a good idea to have written permission before acquiring or disclosing any personal medical information.

Playground Safety

All states are required to adopt laws regulating playgrounds operated by public agencies. In most states, these laws apply to child care centers, but in many states family child care is exempt. However, a growing number of states are adopting laws pertaining to family child care. In addition, many family child care licensing organizations require providers to adhere to specific playground standards before they will issue a license. You should know the applicable laws so you can check for safety on your visits.

Lead Paint

Know the laws about lead paint and lead paint screening in your state. Most states require a child to be screened at several ages. Some states require family child care homes to be certified as lead-paint free. In other states, family child care homes must disclose the presence of any lead paint to the parents.

Maintain Confidentiality

Confidentiality can raise legal issues. Confidentiality issues are varied and complex; here we discuss just a few of the issues that are important to home visitors. For example, your reports could be subpoenaed for a claim against a provider or parent. Let's look at an example.

Scenario

A child is injured. A few months later, when it becomes apparent the child will have a scar, the parent decides to sue the provider. The provider claims that the child did not attend her facility on the date of the injury. The mother states that the child did attend child care on that date.

YOUR ROLE

The court could subpoena your attendance reports for that time period. What are your legal rights and obligations? Check with your administrator. Most organizations include a clause in the provider contract that allows release of information for purposes such as this. If there is no such clause, contact the provider to get a signed release for the information.

This scenario demonstrates why you need to know which governmental or regulatory agencies you are authorized to share information with. If you are unsure, seek the legal counsel of your organization or go to your personal attorney.

• • • • • • • • •

Confidentiality can also become an issue when a provider reveals information to you. In one of our case studies, Tanya told Lila up front that she could not promise confidentiality until she heard what Lila had to say. Whenever a provider or a parent says, "Promise you won't tell anyone . . ." or "Don't say I told you this, but . . ." you should immediately let her know that you cannot promise confidentiality without first hearing what she has to tell you.

Confidentiality is also important because of the types of written information you handle as a home visitor. Documents, personal information, and reports should all be kept in a safe place. Never leave these items out for others to see. Confidentiality about a child or family extends to oral transmission and new technologies. Information given on the telephone, by e-mail, via text messaging, or through any other medium must be protected. Digital images have become a new area of sensitivity. Publishing any image of a child in any medium without permission from parents is a breach of confidentiality. Printing images of children without identifying them by name is not allowed either. Some providers are very experienced with computers and print their own advertising flyers or pamphlets with pictures of children in their child care, or they post images on social networks. Providers should always have written permission that specifically states what the pictures will be used for. They must keep the signed permission slips in their files.

Remember That You Are Visiting Private Homes

When making home visits, you should always carry identification that shows you are an employee of your organization. The identification can be a badge or a card. It should include your picture, name, and the organization you represent. Your ID should also include the organization's address and phone number so your employment can be verified. Because you are entering private homes, you should never feel offended when you are asked to prove your identity.

Once you enter a home, adhere carefully to your professional visit. Go only where you are supposed to go within the home. You need to know exactly which rooms in each provider's home are licensed for child care. Going into other areas of the home without permission could have negative consequences for you. Examine the following situations, which could raise legal issues for home visitors during inspections.

Scenario

A home visitor is checking to see if child safety locks have been installed on the lower cabinets. The home visitor opens the cabinet and finds illegal drugs. The provider could claim that the cabinet was opened without her permission or that the home visitor planted the drugs in the cabinet.

YOUR ROLE

When inspecting refrigerators or cabinets, you should always ask the provider to open the doors.

Scenario

A provider's child care facility is on the basement level. The provider finds it difficult to interrupt her program to take all the children upstairs to answer the door. She has told the home visitor, "Just let yourself in and come down to the child care area." For many months, the home visitor has entered the home and proceeded downstairs. It has worked well. Then the home visitor makes an unannounced visit. She enters the home and proceeds down to the lower level. She finds the provider out of compliance; too many children are present. The home visitor cites the provider for not being in compliance with state regulations. Receiving the citation means that the provider's license and reimbursement for child care services may be in jeopardy. The provider sues the home visitor and her organization, saying the home visitor entered without permission. She further states that if the home visitor had knocked, she would not have opened the door; consequently, she would not have received the citation.

YOUR ROLE

Protect yourself and your organization from legal expenses by creating good documentation. You need documentation of the provider's request and permission to enter the home unannounced. The documentation should include the date, specific information, such as under what circumstances you may enter the home without knocking, and signatures of all parties. Legal counsel should review the document to assure it covers all and any situations that may apply.

In deciding to adopt this policy, other facts should be considered. There is the danger that something could be missing on the day of your visit, and you could be accused of stealing. You could walk into an inappropriate situation involving another family member who was unaware that you had entered. Discuss whether or not you want to adopt this policy at all with your supervisors.

Scenario

Occasionally a provider may ask you to supervise the children while she leaves the room to attend to something. Later the provider could claim that a child was injured while were supervising.

YOUR ROLE

To protect yourself, you should not allow yourself to be placed in a situation where you are alone with the children. You should make sure you are not left alone, which could allow a provider to claim that you stole something. For example, she might need to leave the room to take the children to the bathroom. If you notice that she has left her purse on the table, ask her to take it with her.

 ## CHECKPOINT—Legal Resource File

Home visitors should develop a legal resource file about issues that providers may face. Your resource file should contain documents on specific laws and where they can be found. States laws vary, and you should be familiar with your state's laws. The following checklist suggests the copies of documents you should keep in your resource file:

☐ Your state's licensing requirements

☐ Your state's mandated reporting laws

☐ Your organization's procedures for mandated reporting

☐ Cell phone usage laws while operating a moving vehicle

☐ Your organization's cell phone policy

☐ Documentation for permission to enter a provider's home unannounced

☐ Laws pertaining to medical disclosure, including HIV/AIDS

☐ Laws pertaining to lead paint

☐ Laws pertaining to playground safety

☐ Checklist of documentation pertaining to child custody issues and restraining orders that providers should keep in their files

☐ List of who has the legal right to view your records

☐ Other state laws that apply to you or your clients

Module 11

....

Take Good Notes

Module Description
· ·

This module deals with one of the most important responsibilities of a home visitor: the ability to take clear, concise, and accurate notes. You are a conduit for information you receive during a visit and are required to communicate to your employer. You also impart information from your employer to the provider. It is important that the information collected and conveyed be accurate and reliable.

Home visitors are frequently in a position to have your documentation reviewed by many people. On occasion your information may become the basis for legal action or action taken against a license. With stakes like these, reliability and clarity become paramount. This module contains guidelines to help you produce reliable documents.

Learning Objectives

- Understand the importance of accurate documentation.
- Establish and maintain good documentation skills.

· · · · · · · · ·

Case Study
· ·

Lu is retiring from her position as a home visitor. She has been monitoring homes for many years and has visited hundreds of providers. Now it's time to transfer her files to the home visitor who will be taking her place.

Lu has a great deal of respect for the providers she has visited and come to know. She hopes that the home visitor who takes on these cases can read her files and understand the quality of care that takes place in most of these family child care homes. Lu also hopes that the new home visitor can easily identify clients who need additional attention and targeted assistance based on her documentation. Lu has providers in her caseload who require more observation than others, and she wants the new home visitor to be able to identify those clients easily.

As Lu reviews her folders one last time, she feels confident that she has included enough information in each file so that anyone reading it gets an accurate picture without her being present. Lu has used concise language. Her notes are neat and legibly written, her language is clear and factual. Any abbreviations Lu has used in her documentation are easily understood by anyone reading them. She has attempted to keep her notes brief and to the point so a reader can focus on the important issues almost immediately. Any information received from sources other than the provider or Lu has been clearly identified. Any cited noncompliances are clearly identified as well, and the corrective action plan can be easily reviewed.

After reviewing her files, Lu is confident that the new home visitor will have an accurate and readily accessible history of the providers who have been in Lu's caseload. She is happy that her caseload is represented in an honest and straightforward manner. She feels better about her retirement knowing that the person who will assume her caseload already has a sufficient amount of accurate base information.

· · · · · · · · ·

Note-Taking

To adequately support any assessments you make, you must effectively document what you have observed during your visits. Every evaluation should be substantiated with your documentation. Good documentation provides accountability for you and allows you to paint an accurate and impartial picture of your home visits. In many instances, you are the eyes and ears of your agency. Because quality child care involves many components, your documentation must be comprehensive and cover all the relevant pieces of the picture.

Regardless of the reliability of your memory, notes are an important component of good documentation. Good note-taking makes your job easier.

When you take careful notes during a visit, you are presenting an image of professional accountability to the person you are visiting. When you use good listening skills and ask a provider for clarification before putting your pen to paper, you demonstrate your willingness to document accurately. Good note-taking is especially valuable when you are making several visits in one day. Your notes should help you organize your thoughts and re-create an accurate picture of each and every home visit, even on the busiest day.

When taking notes, you should try to reproduce the conversation that occurred. You should note what you share with the provider as well as how the provider responds to your statements and questions. Occasionally, and certainly should an investigation occur, a provider might try to deny that you made her aware of relevant information. Although not foolproof, your documentation written at the time of a visit, accurately reporting any and all information shared with the provider, can be very helpful. Some home visitors take the precaution of asking providers to initial their notes or their data collection tools before they leave the child care area. This protects providers and home visitors from any subsequent misunderstandings about what actually took place during a visit.

Creating good documentation is an acquired skill. The more you use and develop your writing skills, the more proficient you will become. Creating data collection tools with your supervisor can also assist you in collecting relevant and focused information that you can later convert to useful documentation.

When you create notes during a visit to a provider's home, remember that you are representing your organization. Your notes should be professional. Remember that in most instances the notes you take during a visit can be subject to subpoena. That means that many people may see what you have written. Do not include anything in your notes that you would not want another professional to read. For example, demeaning comments do not belong in your notes. Don't exaggerate or sensationalize information because it makes you look more important; this does a disservice to the provider as well as to yourself.

Perhaps you remember the children's game Gossip or Operator. One child quietly tells a story, and that story is repeated down the line of children. At the end, the story that results from repeated tellings is compared to the original story. Usually the end result is a story that bears little resemblance to the story initially told. Don't make your notes a vehicle for this type of distortion. There is no need to embellish the facts, not even a little bit. This is especially important when a problem does occur. Your documentation needs to be accurate representation of what actually occurred. When taking notes, answer the following questions with specific facts:

- Who was involved? This includes the names and ages of everyone present and their connection to the family child care program.
- What actually occurred? Note the specific chronology of events, including how you obtained this information if you were not an eyewitness.
- Where did it occur? Write the time, date, address, room, and where in the room—for example, "in high chair," "under table."
- How did the event occur? Write down the provider's explanation and any other explanations from people involved, such as parents, children, or other people visiting the facility.

Remember to clearly differentiate between the information that comes from your own observations and that learned from others. Do not incorporate someone else's opinion and present it as your own.

Tips for Taking Notes

When you are on a routine visit, taking notes should be a natural part of your job. Taking notes begins with physical preparation. Make note-taking a part of your routine by standardizing it:

- Develop and use a standard method of note-taking. Always start with the provider's name and date on each page. Standardize punctuation, abbreviations, and margins. Make your original notes legible enough so you can read them, but use abbreviations of your own when possible. Be careful with them—use only those you are comfortable with and can easily translate later, when you document. When in doubt, write it out.
- Take and keep notes in a notebook. The effort required to recopy notes from loose papers is better spent in rereading and thinking about them. You might choose to use a large loose-leaf notebook, which allows you to add or remove pages. A large notebook also offers wide margins for indenting and outlining. A small notebook is easier to carry.
- Leave a few blank spaces. White space between topics gives you room to fill in additional points later.

- Write with ink. Use pen, not pencil, for permanency.
- Draw sketches. Sketching helps some people remember details accurately. This can be especially helpful when you are attempting to convey the layout or floor plan of a child care setting. Consider taking photographs, perhaps with your cell phone. You should consult your supervisor about this possibility. For more about taking photographs, see module 10.
- Complete all notes as soon as possible after the home visit. You should document information while it is fresh in your mind. On any given day, you may make several visits; keeping your information straight is especially important when you are visiting more than one home.

Be sure that you have a way to take notes while you are engaged with a client. You certainly should not focus all of your attention on note-taking, but you do need to create good records. Here are some helpful tips:

- Listen actively. When you double-check your understanding of what you hear, you show respect. This also gives you time to think before you write, ensuring greater accuracy.
- Try to be as open-minded as possible about points with which you disagree. Don't let disagreement interfere with your note-taking. Remember that your notes should be an accurate record of what happened. If you are feeling too emotional about an issue or a discussion that has occurred, you probably cannot document the discussion in a nonbiased way. If you feel that the circumstances of the visit do not allow you to document objectively, you should contact your supervisor immediately.
- Spend most of your time listening and observing. Take notes only on the main points. If you are constantly writing, you cannot be a very discriminating listener or observer. Not everything is of equal importance. Focus on the main things that happen or are discussed.
- Have a system in place for organizing and storing your notes. You have put thought and effort into taking good notes; don't minimize that effort by being too casual with them.
    - Never throw away your notes. When you remove your notes from your notebook, store them with your work papers.

- ○ Don't ignore your notes. Use them when you are documenting your home visits.
- ○ Keep a copy of any previous home visit notes in your provider folder. This helps ensure that you will remember to offer any necessary follow-up.

The Importance of Being Objective

When you take notes, accuracy is important. You should use your notes to create your documentation. Whenever you draw a conclusion about a provider's performance, you need to support your conclusion with your records of observation. You should not attempt to substantiate your conclusions after the fact. If, for example, you return to your office and find a comment about unsanitary conditions in your notes, you should also find something in the notes explaining what occurred to make you come to that conclusion. Your conclusion should not be based on personal opinion but on what you actually observed or experienced during your home visit.

Occasionally you may feel uncomfortable and concerned about a home based more on your instincts than on anything specific that you observed. Discuss your concerns with your supervisor. Be extremely cautious about including anything in your written documentation that you are unable to substantiate.

Accurate documentation is based in part on a fair and impartial assessment. Much of your credibility comes from your ability to maintain objectivity when developing documentation and assessments. Many components of a home visit can be easily documented—for example, if the trash receptacle is uncovered and accessible to children or if the exits are blocked. You can generally determine if specific noncompliances indicate a larger pattern of marginal behavior through ongoing observation and note-taking over a period of time. Your documentation creates a history that will reveal a pattern of noncompliance if there is one. The cumulative history may demonstrate reasons for concern that a single visit may not.

Obviously, your assessments can have a serious impact on a provider's ability to operate a successful child care business. For this reason, your ability to create a clear and concise chronology based on the observations you make during your home visit is essential. Make sure to check and double-check your notes and facts. When in doubt about any conclusion you draw, you might choose to revisit the home or call the client or other relevant sources of information for clarification.

CHECKPOINT—Note-Taking

Use this list when you review your notes.

Are your notes accurate?	YES │ NO
Did you repeat information back for accuracy?	YES │ NO
Did you verify the spelling of names?	YES │ NO
Are your notes brief and concise?	YES │ NO
Did you use common abbreviations?	YES │ NO
Are your notes clearly written and easily understood?	YES │ NO
Did you write legibly?	YES │ NO
Are your notes organized?	YES │ NO
Are your notes complete?	YES │ NO

Collect Data Efficiently

Module Description

Home visitors need to be prepared to accurately record what they observe during a visit then use what they recorded to compile accurate documentation. Depending on your organization's mandate, your monitoring duties may be extensive. Use tools that help you collect all the necessary information in an organized way. Doing so allows you to complete a home visit in a reasonable amount of time as well as to communicate information obtained during the visit in an organized and understandable fashion.

This module provides you with sample assessment tools. It also provides helpful information about establishing compliance procedures and collecting relevant and reliable resource material.

Learning Objectives

- Be able to collect all required information quickly and efficiently.
- Create and maintain a system to document each home visitor–client interaction.
- Create and use efficient data collection tools.

· · · · · · · ·

Case Study

As Colleen reviews her schedule of visits for the following day, one name catches her attention. She recalls that Emma phoned a few weeks ago, requesting

157

some resource information. Colleen cannot recall exactly what Emma wanted. In preparation for the visit, Colleen pulls out the client's file. When she checks the contact sheet, she sees that Emma has requested some technical assistance on menu planning. Colleen realizes that she is now committed to bringing the information with her for tomorrow's visit. By reviewing the folder, Colleen saves herself the embarrassment of telling Emma she has forgotten her promise. Colleen locates the resource material and delivers it to the provider.

Emma is happy to see Colleen and delighted to receive the information she requested. During the visit, Colleen uses data collection tools that allow her to walk around the child care environment and observe while at the same time collecting necessary information. Because her data collection tools are comprehensive and well-organized, Colleen is able to complete her visit efficiently. Emma is grateful for this, because she wants to take the children outside, and everyone has been patiently waiting for the visit to end. Colleen can discuss with Emma any issues that have arisen as a result of her review, because her data collection tools allow both her and Emma ready access to any noncompliance issues. Colleen completes her visit to everyone's satisfaction and arrives at her next visit on time and well prepared.

Both Colleen and Emma are happy with the manner in which this visit was conducted. Emma received the information she had requested, and Colleen feels especially pleased that she could retrieve all the required information while reinforcing her collaborative working relationship with Emma.

The Importance of Data Collection Tools

As stated throughout this manual, home visiting, although rewarding, can also be very challenging. Rarely can you enter a home when children are awake and active and conduct your visits without numerous interruptions. Sometimes it is very difficult to stay focused amid all the distractions of a typical early child care setting. If you combine these factors with the occasional client who cannot or will not focus on the purpose of the visit, accomplishing your objectives can be an uphill battle.

One of the most efficient ways to stay to the point and collect necessary information is to use organized, professional data collection tools. Before conducting a home visit, review the following information:

- Ask yourself what you are in the home to accomplish. What information is necessary for you to obtain during this visit? Are there materials you should be providing or information you should be communicating to the provider? Are there specific objectives for your visit (for example, are you following up on a complaint, checking enrollment, providing curriculum assistance)?
- Whom are you visiting? Are you aware of the provider's licensing history? Are there specific things or individuals you should be looking for, such as overenrollment or a disqualified household member?
- Are there any special circumstances? Have you been requested by your organization to share new regulatory or contractual information, for example?

What follows are a variety of data collection tools that can assist you in collecting necessary information in an organized fashion. The examples provided are generic. Use them to create tools to support your organization's specific requirements.

Contact Sheet

As we have discussed throughout this manual, the more relevant information you have about the individuals and the programs you visit, the better off you are. A contact sheet that stays in each client's folder is very helpful. It helps you maintain an ongoing record of your interactions with a client, including telephone conversations. Each new contact sheet should contain the provider's name, address, and phone number. Each entry should be dated and initialed. The contact sheet gives anyone who reads the file important information that is organized chronologically.

The contact sheet is an appropriate place for you to record anecdotal information after a visit. It can also be used when a client calls and has requests or questions. Checking a contact sheet before each visit helps you gather any relevant resources you will need for a follow-up visit. As demonstrated in the case study, a well-organized contact sheet gives you a written record of what you said during a visit or during a telephone conversation. This is helpful when a client tells you, "You never told me that." In keeping an accurate and updated contact sheet, you can refer to that information and tell her that she was indeed given the information—and even provide the date on which she was given it.

Sample Contact Sheet

Provider: Mary Jones

Address: 123 Elm Street
Anywhere, US, 12345

Phone Number: 222-555-1234

Date	Interaction
5/15/10	Mary called requesting new menus. I told her menus would be sent today. MG (the home visitor's initials).

Tools for Collecting Data

When developing collection tools, you should first determine what information you are attempting to obtain. The most important evidence of appropriate child care is always the well-being of the children enrolled in the program. Depending on your particular job duties, you may be looking at one specific aspect of the program or you may be in the home to monitor all aspects of the child care setting. Four main areas of observation can assist you in creating your evaluation tools: health and safety, age-appropriate materials and curriculum, appropriate business practices, and a provider's demonstrated ability to offer appropriate child care.

When assessing an entire family child care environment, you should look closely at all aspects of a program. Using efficient data collection tools helps you to quickly determine areas that need further attention and discussion while providing an opportunity to reinforce your positive observations.

In creating tools that work for you, think about the routine you usually follow during your home visits. Create a data collection tool that reflects each step you take during your visits. We have included four samples in this module as references, recognizing that you understand the expectations of your visits better than anyone else. Custom-tailor a data collection tool so that it works effectively for you. Provide ample room to record your observations.

Remember that any assessment tool should include space for client information. The provider's name, address, and telephone number should always be included. Space for licensing information, such as a license number and expiration date, should also be included when required.

Data Collection on Health and Safety

Health and safety are paramount in every child care environment. Using tools that help you maintain a record of what you see during your home visits not only protects your credibility, but in some cases the health and safety of enrolled children. Your assessment tool should offer sufficient space to include projected time frames for a provider to correct any documented noncompliances.

Some health and safety issues cannot wait for a follow-up visit. Those noncompliances should be corrected immediately, if possible, and the correction noted during your visit. Some examples include blocked exits, smoke and carbon detectors that don't work, or hazards that are accessible to young children.

Health and Safety Assessment

Provider: _____

Address: _____

_____

Phone number: _____

License #: _____   Expiration date: _____

Sanitation (all areas used by children) _____

_____

_____

Accessible hazards (inside and outside) _____

_____

_____

_____

Exits _____

_____

_____

Working detectors (smoke and carbon monoxide) _____

_____

_____

Health and Safety Assessment (continued)

Overall maintenance (note things such as peeling paint, broken steps or railings)

_____

_____

_____

Required safety equipment (gates for stairs, safety locks, outlet barriers)

_____

_____

_____

Secure windows and appropriate placement of furniture

_____

_____

_____

Regularly scheduled safety drills _____

_____

_____

Sufficient equipment and materials that are in good repair

_____

_____

_____

Data Collection on Age-Appropriate Curriculum

In most states, licensed providers are required to offer age-appropriate activities for the children in their care. Children in child care should not be sitting in front of TVs for extended periods of time, for example. Establishing appropriate curriculum for groups of multiage children is challenging. Family child care programs, however, still need to adequately meet the needs of all enrolled children.

Your data collections tools should allow you to efficiently observe a program to determine if each age group has access to toys and materials that meet their developmental needs. You should also pay close attention to the physical environment to determine if the developmental needs of infants, toddlers, and preschoolers are being met. For example, is the provider using all of her licensed space, or is she confining children to one small room? Do infants have access to protected and clean floor space where they can stretch, exercise, and have tummy time? Toddlers, who are in many ways all about gross motor skill development, need open and usable space to walk, run, and skip. Does the child care setting provide that space and those opportunities? Preschoolers need areas for quiet as well as active activities. Are these needs being adequately addressed?

Age-Appropriate Curriculum Assessment

Provider: _____

Address: _____

_____

Phone number: _____

License #: _____   Expiration date: _____

Inclusive and appropriate daily schedule of activities for each participating age group

_____

_____

Sufficient and age-appropriate materials and equipment

_____

_____

Physical environment that meets the developmental needs of each participating child

_____

_____

Examples of applied curriculum

_____

_____

Provider demonstrates the ability to assess the effectiveness of her curriculum

_____

Data Collection on Ability to Care

Your obligation as a home visitor very often includes your ability to evaluate a provider's ability to offer appropriate child care. This is often the most difficult assessment you will make. Some family child care homes are well organized and have an abundance of materials and equipment, but the provider for a variety of reasons is not equipped to offer quality child care. Some providers are under a great deal of stress because of the loss of a loved one, financial problems, or health issues. It is easy to empathize with someone who is experiencing difficulties, but it is also important to remember that your primary objective should always be the well-being of enrolled children.

You should remember objectivity is required when assessing a provider's ability to care. Rely on your knowledge of regulatory requirements and your experience regarding best practices in early child care settings. As we have discussed throughout this manual, your conclusions need to be adequately supported by your observations and experiences during each visit.

Ability to Care Assessment

Provider: _____

Address: _____

_____

Phone number: _____

License #: _____   Expiration date: _____

Provider's appearance and demeanor

_____

_____

_____

Clean and well-cared for children

_____

_____

_____

Appropriate supervision

_____

_____

_____

Ability to Care Assessment (continued)

Appropriate interaction between provider and children

_____

_____

Provider demonstrates understanding of age-appropriate growth and development

_____

_____

_____

Provider demonstrates good physical and mental health

_____

_____

_____

Provider demonstrates appropriate strategies for guiding behavior

_____

_____

_____

Provider meets all licensing requirements (for example, updated physical, CPR and first aid training requirements)

_____

_____

_____

Data Collection on Appropriate Business Practices

A requirement of your home visits usually includes your ability to determine accountability. You may work for an organization that reimburses providers for the money they spend on food used to feed participating children. You may work for an organization that supplies eligible parents with subsidized child care. As we discussed in module 1, your ability to determine that the services purchased by your organization and by parents have been provided appropriately is very important.

Providers are generally more successful when they are able to operate their businesses in an organized fashion. In most states, licensed providers are required to keep certain information about each child in care. Immunization records, signed permission forms, information regarding allergies, and personality traits are all examples of required record keeping. Required information may also include evacuation logs and accurate time records for staff. Providers who affiliate with a food sponsor are also required to submit attendance records and accurate menus. Providers who enroll children whose parents receive subsidized child care money or vouchers are also required to keep accurate and current attendance records.

Your data collection tool should help you review all required paperwork efficiently and comprehensively. There is nothing quite as frustrating as completing a visit and leaving a home only to remember later in the day that you overlooked paperwork you were required to review.

Appropriate Business Practices Assessment

Provider: _____

Address: _____

_____

Phone number: _____

License #: _____   Expiration date: _____

☐ Child care information for each child (check to make sure you know what is required in your state or by your organization)

☐ Updated health and immunization records (when applicable for the provider as well as all the enrolled children)

☐ Required attendance records

☐ Required menus

☐ Required logs

☐ Current license and expiration dates for provider and approved assistants (when applicable)

☐ Evidence of CPR and first aid (when required)

☐ Evidence of training hours (when required)

☐ Appropriate storage of records to assure confidentiality

☐ Appropriate archiving of records for children no longer in the program for the required amount of time

☐ Evidence of required permits for renovation or wood-burning stoves

☐ Evidence of insurance (when required)

☐ Evidence of driver's license, registration, and automobile insurance (when applicable)

☐ Evidence of licenses for household pets when applicable

Compliance Procedures

You and your organization benefit from the development of appropriate procedures that address compliance violations serious enough to present immediate danger to participating children. A blocked exit, for example, might fall into that category. If the violation can be fixed during the visit, the correction should occur immediately, while you are present. If a violation cannot be corrected, it is strongly recommended that you have a plan in place that you can implement. If a compliance issue is sufficiently serious, the plan should include directions for the protection and possible removal of children.

It is a good practice when you note something to be corrected on your checklist or in your notes, that you immediately make the provider aware of it. Your documentation should be impartial and based on objective observations. The underlying purpose of an effective assessment tool is to provide an organized way to communicate your observations. If the provider is given an objective evaluation, she can make corrections and improvements proactively.

Assessment tools, like notes, should contain summarized information. Use abbreviations and concise language. Sometimes you may have to simply write, "See notes," and then later write a longer summary than your assessment tool allows. If so, remember to attach additional notes to your assessment tool.

Store your visit assessments in an accessible place that makes easy review of information possible. Keep in mind that your professionalism extends to your assessment tools.

Create a Resource File

Every home visitor should have generic resource materials that are readily available to share with clients. Of course, you can't always anticipate what issues will arise during a visit. Remember to make a note regarding requested resources. On occasion a provider may not request a resource, but based on an observation during your visit, you may choose to provide specific resource information.

Be constantly on the lookout for resource materials to bring with you on home visits. Local resource and referral agencies frequently have relevant and current child care information available. Licensing agencies often have useful resource material available on their Web sites. Your local community college may also offer good resource material through its early education program. National organizations such as National Association for the Education of Young Children (www.naeyc.org) and the National Association for Family Child Care (www.nafcc.org) provide relevant information in their newsletters and on their Web sites. The more instructive and relevant the information you can share, the more clients will come to see your visit as an opportunity for assistance rather than as an intrusion.

Remember to personally review and understand any information that you plan to share with clients; you need to feel comfortable with it. You should always check your resource information for accuracy, and you should be prepared to respond to client questions.

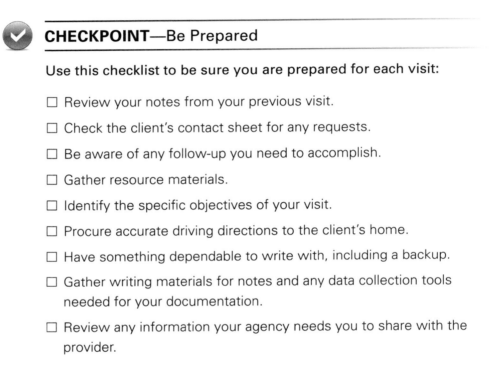

✔ CHECKPOINT—Be Prepared

Use this checklist to be sure you are prepared for each visit:

☐ Review your notes from your previous visit.

☐ Check the client's contact sheet for any requests.

☐ Be aware of any follow-up you need to accomplish.

☐ Gather resource materials.

☐ Identify the specific objectives of your visit.

☐ Procure accurate driving directions to the client's home.

☐ Have something dependable to write with, including a backup.

☐ Gather writing materials for notes and any data collection tools needed for your documentation.

☐ Review any information your agency needs you to share with the provider.

Put Safety First

Module Description
. . . .

Home visiting has many unique aspects that are not common to other professions. As a visitor, you not only enter clients' places of business; but as stated
throughout this manual, you also enter their private homes. In assessing a
strictly commercial environment, you can discuss your conclusions without the
conversation becoming personal. When you visit someone's home, however,
any evaluation or assessment can seem personal and may result in a client behaving defensively.

Workplace safety is a topic that is often overlooked when organizations are
establishing policies for home visitors. The reality is, however, that when you
are visiting homes to monitor services, you never know what is happening on
the other side of the door. It is unwise to assume that because your caseload
is located in an upscale neighborhood, safety is not an important issue. It is
unwise to assume anything. You never know what is happening in a child care
home until you are actually inside and can see for yourself.

You should have a safety plan in mind prior to making any home visit. You
should be proactive in encouraging your administrative staff to develop workplace safety policies if they have not already done so. As this module explains,
your plans should include anticipating and responding to dangers that may
arise from many different scenarios, including unsafe environments, aggressive
people, dangerous pets, and other physical hazards.

Learning Objectives

- Develop and follow safety action plan.
- Understand when and if you should call for assistance.

. . . .

Case Study

Virginia is conducting a monitoring visit in an urban neighborhood that has a history of high crime. Although Virginia has many providers in this neighborhood and visits it frequently, she is always cautious. Because she stays aware and informed, she knows the area has recently experienced numerous car thefts and assaults. Keeping this in mind, she parks in a secure, well-lit parking lot. Virginia has also made herself aware of the location of each exit, and she tries to park in view of both the attendant and an exit.

As Virginia approaches the apartment building where Connie resides, she notices a group of young men and women standing in front of an adjacent building. She remains calm and aware. Rather than walking through this group of people, she chooses to walk around them.

Upon reaching the door to the provider's apartment, Virginia hears loud voices coming from inside. The sound is not coming from children; these are loud adult voices. Virginia can identify one voice as that of Connie, and she thinks the second adult voice may be the voice of Connie's adult son. Connie's son has had a disqualifying criminal background check and has agreed not to be present in the provider's home during child care hours.

After Virginia rings the doorbell, she positions herself to the side of the door rather than directly in front of it. She does this because she is aware that a swinging door can act as a weapon. When the door opens, Connie's adult son appears in the doorway. He is not happy to see Virginia, and he tells her how frustrating it is that he cannot come home during the day because his mother is providing child care in their home. Virginia remains calm. She informs him that she has a scheduled visit with his mother and wants to speak with her. At this point, Connie appears at the door. She is very apologetic. She informs Virginia that her son has just returned home to pick up something he forgot this morning. Connie was upset because she realized Virginia was coming and he was not supposed to be present.

Virginia indicates that she understands what Connie has said; nonetheless, she must document what she has witnessed. She states that she would like to come in and conduct her visit, but Connie's son should not be present. She calmly explains to Connie and her son that a disqualifying background check is outside of her authority. She then calmly shares information about the appeal process and how Connie and her son can approach this issue if they feel the disqualification is unfair. Virginia reiterates that she must conduct her visit and that Connie's son cannot be present. She offers Connie the option of asking her son to leave so Virginia can conduct her visit or of having Virginia return to her office and reschedule the visit.

Connie and her son respond to Virginia's information in a positive way. The son apologizes for being frustrated and indicates that he is returning to work. Virginia is able to conduct her visit. She informs Connie that she will document what she saw and heard, but she will also include Connie's explanation of the events. Virginia conducts her visit and confirms that the environment is calm and suitable for the children present.

The responsibilities of her profession occasionally place Virginia in potentially vulnerable situations. She accepts this and has learned to maintain a high level of awareness when conducting visits. She feels that her ability to maintain a proactive approach helps keep her safe and allows her to do her job effectively. This knowledge helps Virginia feel satisfied with the outcome of her visit to Connie's home.

· · · · · · · · ·

Make a Safety Action Plan

As a professional who conducts home visits, you need to be aware of your personal safety. Keeping safe is a basic necessity for anyone who monitors a variety of homes in many different types of neighborhoods. Entering someone else's personal space and sharing information that may not be well received may place you in a hostile environment. As a result, you need to develop strategies for reducing the likelihood of personal harm.

Being prepared is an important element in feeling safe. If you do not already have a safety action plan, you should create one before scheduling your next visit. Your plan should include precautions to help you avoid dangerous situations:

- Know the neighborhoods where you are required to visit.
- Identify safe areas to park.

- When possible, avoid areas that do not have sufficient lighting or security.
- Have appropriate driving directions and a well-maintained vehicle or quick access to reliable public transportation when applicable.
- Make sure someone in your organization knows your visit schedule.

To create a reliable plan, you need to be able to respond to each situation quickly and appropriately. Before leaving the office for a visit, review the information in your file. Have there been any negative interactions with representatives from your organization in the past? Have you had any history of negative interactions with the person you are planning to visit? Think about the street, neighborhood, and area you are visiting. Use good judgment; for example, avoid wearing jewelry in isolated or high-crime areas. No matter where you are going, make sure your car has sufficient gas and is in good working order. Carrying a cell phone is also a valuable precautionary measure.

Predict Behaviors

Some circumstances can easily result in a negative response. For example, if the tone of your visit results in the client's fear, humiliation, boredom, or sense of powerlessness, those feelings can become an emotional trigger. If your client is exhausted, uses drugs or alcohol, has a physical disability or lives in chronic pain, these emotional triggers can also result in a negative response. Be aware so you can make proactive decisions. During visits, you should always be aware of the body language of all the individuals present:

- Is the person pacing or fidgeting, clenching her fists or jaw?
- Is the person out of touch with reality, speaking loudly, and/or becoming verbally abusive?

If you see these behaviors, take steps to reduce the tension.

Reducing Tension

There is no automatic remedy to reduce tension. First and foremost, if you can, help the angry person calm down. To do this, you must remain calm yourself. A calm tone, demeanor, and presence can be transferred to others. Speak in a clear and direct manner so the person can hear what you are saying in spite of her anger. Avoid saying, "Calm down." When you issue that command, you imply that you do not understand the individual's right to or justification for anger. Try to be empathetic. Talk about the source of frustration or anger, and reflect feelings by using phrases like "You seem angry." If you have made a mistake, take responsibility for it.

Sometimes it is easier to remain calm when you recognize that the client's anger or frustration is not about you—rather, the client is angry about her situation. This realization should prevent defensiveness on your part.

As you work to defuse tension, be sure to reinforce your calm tone with nonthreatening, nonconfrontational body language:

- Move slowly.
- Avoid putting your hands on your hips.
- Position yourself to the side of the client so you aren't squarely facing her.
- Avoid extensive eye contact and physical closeness.
- Never touch an angry person.
- Try not to stand between the person and the door.
- Offer choices, such as talking later or agreeing to a cooling-off period.
- Allow the person to save face by giving her a way out.

Even when someone appears to be calming down, be patient. It takes a person about thirty to forty minutes to calm down physiologically from anger (Griffin, Montsinger, and Carter 1995). Remember that you are always in a position to leave the child care setting, but the children are not. Do not leave a provider in an emotional state that may compromise the safety of children.

If Aggression Occurs

Sometimes a person becomes volatile so quickly that you do not have time to try to defuse the anger. At times a person may even become physically aggressive. Should this happen and you are unable to escape, here are things you can do to defend yourself.

- Protect yourself from head injuries; block blows with your arms or a clipboard.
- If you fall, block the attacker with your feet and legs.
- If your arm is grabbed, break the hold by twisting quickly toward the person's thumb.
- If you are choked, raise both arms straight up and quickly turn around. Your arms and shoulders will break the hold.
- If you are bitten, push into the bite; don't pull away.

- If your hair is pulled, press down on the person's hand with both of yours.

Understand Your Role in Your Personal Safety

Critical self-assessment is important when you are conducting home visits. Ask yourself the following questions:

- Do you misuse your authority?
- Do you give orders rather than share information?
- Do you feel somehow superior to the clients you visit?

If you answered yes to any of these questions, you need to seriously consider making changes to effectively and safely do your job.

There are two important aspects to be aware of during potentially tense situations:

How You Present Yourself

People who are uncomfortable communicating an unpopular message sometimes take refuge in a persona that is stiff and unapproachable. Stiff and unapproachable are not characteristics that lend themselves to good communication. What is your style? Try to incorporate as many empathetic characteristics as you can.

The case study described how Virginia was able to remain calm throughout her visit. She conveyed to Connie and her son that she was listening to what they had to say. She also stayed to the point. By acknowledging the son's frustration, Virginia responded empathetically and professionally. She remained impartial and did not seem judgmental. She provided options to her client. In doing so, Virginia demonstrated her respect for Connie's home and empowered Connie by giving her options.

Being Flexible

When rules are open to interpretation and there is an opportunity for flexibility, do you utilize that opportunity? If your approach can be best described as rigid, do you apply that same standard to every home you visit, or only the homes you see as problematic? If providers sense or hear that you demonstrate different types of behaviors in different homes, your credibility as an effective home visitor can be tarnished. You may also contribute to a more hostile environment in some of the homes you monitor. Create a visit style that you can employ consistently in every home you visit.

The very fact you are entering someone's home as a monitor, which implies authority and accountability, can create a certain amount of tension from the onset. Develop strategies that allow you to communicate all types of feedback effectively while showing respect for your client and her environment. Empathizing and engaging in cooperative problem solving will go a long way to decrease tension and promote your personal safety.

Respond to Pets

More than 4.7 million people each year are bitten by dogs. There are many documented cases of home visitors being injured by household pets. There are no accurate records identifying the number of dogs by breed involved in attacks; consequently, you can't know which breeds are most likely to be aggressive. You should be aware of any dog, regardless of breed, in the homes you visit. Follow these basic rules when entering a home in which a dog is present:

- Do not approach an unfamiliar dog.
- Do not run from a dog.
- Remain still when approached by an unfamiliar dog.
- If knocked over by a dog, roll into a ball and lie still.
- Do not play with a dog unless the owner is present and gives you permission to do so.
- Avoid direct eye contact with a dog.
- Do not disturb a dog that is sleeping, eating, or caring for puppies.
- Do not pet a dog without allowing it to see and sniff you first.

If you are bitten, you should get medical assistance immediately. If possible, obtain proof that the dog is licensed and has appropriate immunization. In some states, all pets in a regulated child care facility must be licensed. If the owner of the animal is unable to supply you with evidence of immunization, contact the authorities and share that information with your physician or emergency room personnel.

Dogs can be very sensitive to tension-charged environments. Dogs are also generally protective of their owners. Remaining calm and communicating information in moderate tones is always helpful, especially when animals are present.

Dogs are not the only pets that may present safety hazards. Be familiar with any pet in a child care environment that you visit. Do your homework. Check with your local health department about pets that may pose health as well as safety hazards. Familiarize yourself with any licensing restrictions that pertain to pets. Bring good resource materials to support providers in meeting requirements.

Document Events

Proactive behavior includes sharing pertinent information that can help protect other professionals who may visit a client's home. If an incident occurs in the course of your visit, you must document it in her file as quickly as possible, while the specifics are still fresh in your mind. Write a clearly worded statement about any incident or circumstance that creates an unsafe environment.

Trust Your Instincts

There are some situations in which you feel uncomfortable; there are other situations in which you feel endangered. There is obviously a difference between the two. You can try to deal with uncomfortable situations, but you should remove yourself from dangerous ones and then immediately take appropriate action to protect the children present in the home.

If being in a certain home or neighborhood or being around a particular client makes you feel uncomfortable, try to determine why. Once you have identified the source of your discomfort, you can begin to develop a strategy for minimizing it. This might be as simple as giving yourself permission to leave the setting and reschedule the visit at a time when the provider is calmer. If there is a household member who is always present during your visits and who behaves confrontationally, you might determine that it is necessary to request that the provider meet with you at a time when the two of you are better able to talk alone. Perhaps there are situations where you feel it is necessary to be accompanied by another person. Find out whether or not your agency has a procedure to provide for this type of peer support. When developing an agency policy two questions that should be addressed are:

- What do you do if you feel your safety or the safety of children is threatened?
- Under what circumstances should the police be called?

If your organization has no plan, suggest that one be developed with staff involvement. Once a plan is in place, all personnel should receive appropriate training.

Because of the nature of your work, you may also face workplace safety issues as a result of hazards in the homes and neighborhoods you visit. These include things such as icy or snowy walkways, broken stairs or porches, and falling debris. Environments that are used for the care of children should be hazard free, but unfortunately they aren't always hazard free. Be prepared to address these types of safety issues with your clients immediately. Do not be shy about pointing out any hazards that compromise your personal safety. Remember—if the physical environment makes you feel unsafe, what is its potential for injury to a child?

Trust your instincts. One of the results of visiting lots of homes is developing an instinct about what is a safe or unsafe environment. Unfortunately, you cannot always anticipate safety issues. That is why you must always be prepared.

 CHECKPOINT—Your Safety

Follow these general precautions for every home visit so you are prepared and able to protect your safety:

- Drive by a residence before you conduct a visit. This will give you the opportunity to observe the immediate area.

- When driving into a parking lot, look to see if anyone is loitering and what the mood seems to be. Note at least two exits from the parking lot, and back your car in when possible.

- When you approach the home, listen for any disturbances like yelling that are not normal sounds in a child care environment.

- When knocking at a door, stand to the side. Do not put yourself in a position where the door can be used as a means for a provider or household member to injure you.

- Always introduce yourself and state clearly why you are visiting the home.

- Assess the demeanor of the person answering the door.

- Know where the exits are located in the home.

- Be sure the staff at your organization know where you are when you conduct a home visit.

- Know when and how to conclude a visit and leave the premises to defuse a tense situation.

References

Delude, Cathryn. 2009. Adult brain can change within seconds. *MIT News,* July 14, 2009. http://web.mit.edu/newsoffice/2009/blindspot-0714 .html.

Griffin, William V., Montsinger, James L., and Carter, Nancy A. 1995. *Resource guide on personal safety for administrators and other personnel.* Durham, NC: Brendan Associates and ILR.

Knowles, Malcolm S. 1970. *The modern practice of adult education: Andragogy versus pedagogy.* Chicago: Follett.

Phipps, Robert. 2008. Body language facts and stats. http://www.robert-phipps.com/articles/body-language-facts-and-stats.html.

Shindler, John. 2009. *Transformative classroom management: Positive strategies to engage all students and promote a psychology of success.* San Francisco: Jossey-Bass.

Soukhanov, Anne, ed. 1999. *Encarta world English dictionary.* New York: St. Martin's Press.